THE LUCKY GENERATION

The Life, Loves and Times of a (Slightly Mad) Baby Boomer

By Brian R Sumner

authorHOUSE®

AuthorHouse™ UK Ltd.
500 Avebury Boulevard
Central Milton Keynes, MK9 2BE
www.authorhouse.co.uk
Phone: 08001974150

Published by AuthorHouse   4/3/2013

ISBN: 978-1-4567-7921-4 (sc)
ISBN: 978-1-4567-7922-1 (e)

TABLE OF CONTENTS

CHAPTER ONE
PROLOGUE

First let me just say that everything I"m going to tell you is the absolute truth. Well I would say that wouldn"t I, but it is. I"ve always found the truth goes a long way in life and anyway, as it happens, I"ve never been a very good liar. *I am Brian Sumner*, one of the "Lucky Generation" known as the "Baby Boomers ". This is my story and the story of my generation covering my take on the story of our post war World to the present day. Amongst other things it"s a story of real life with its hope and despair, its loves, infidelities and betrayals, compromises, trials and triumphs, along with those "two imposters, success and failure " during a seismic period in the history of our planet.

> *"Remember there is nothing stable in human affairs, therefore avoid undue elation in prosperity or undue depression in adversity"*
>
> *Socrates*

I awake. Its 2.35am, February 1985. I feel like shit. I expect I look like shit as is usual these days. I"m getting desperate. I wake every morning at about 2.35am, and I"m not going to get back to sleep until thoroughly exhausted early the next morning and maybe not even then. Then I have to get up and go to work. Its a familiar pattern that is developing, but a very strange and frightening one and something is very wrong with me, but I don"t yet have a clue what other than its associated with my worries. This whole thing has now been going on for several months and is getting worse. It doesn"t seem to matter what time I went to bed, or even how many drinks I have consumed or not consumed. It"s a pattern I can"t seem to break. What I do know is I"m very worried about something and I know what that something is.

Night after night I had lain awake, unable to keep still, tossing and turning into the small hours. I have the radio on at all times for company. I get up during the night and smoke cigarette after cigarette, then collapse in bed hours later exhausted and STILL can"t sleep. I feel generally agitated and anxious - I can"t concentrate on anything other than how I FEEL which is not good. Confusion, lapse of memory and failure of mental focus follow. Thinking, thinking. Days then weeks drifting by. I felt ill but not in a way I had ever experienced before. I went to the Doctor and he diagnoses depression and puts me on something but with no positive improvement. Nothing I did seemed to bring any joy to my life. My self esteem and my self confidence then disappeared altogether to be replaced by a general feeling of worthlessness. I looked and felt miserable. Relief was spasmodic and fleeting. Let me tell you a serious depression is not as basic as just feeling a bit pissed off, a feeling of the "Blues". Its much, much more than that. I was in a catatonic state. It was very frightening indeed and I wasn"t functioning properly. I was a dozy pillock at work, my mind was definitely not on the job, and I was doing a very important job with much at stake. Everything took on a negative slant. I was experiencing considerable anguish. Then my Libido disappeared. Eventually I was sent to a Psychiatrist. The Psychiatrist tells me I am experiencing what he called "Event depression " . Unhappily I generally derived little or no benefit from these "Consultations". The "Event " was clearly the breakdown of my marriage a year or more before, following which we decided to split and I would go down to London to work, exacerbated by the stress of the project I had gone down there to complete. The depression had not yet gone "Clinical " but things were heading that way.

Depression: "A chemical in-balance amidst the neurotransmitters in the Brain, possibly the result of systemic stress causing a depletion of chemicals serotonin and norepinephrine ". Author William Styron, himself a victim of this illness, in his excellent book "Darkness Visible", describes it as a disruption to the "Circadian cycle", the metabolic and glandular rhythms central to our lives. The brain gets confused and starts giving out the wrong messages. Judgement is severely impaired.

Logical and reliable thought no longer possible. The libido and appetite disappear. Instances of anxiety become more frequent. Unhappily, outsiders and observers are unable to grasp the essence of the illness making it difficult for them to help even if they wanted to. Some are unsympathetic. They begin to keep away. Some chat and lots of Pills follows. Lots of Bills. The "Anti- depressants " and "sleeping " pills I was taking did not make one jot of difference. Maybe making me worse? Later studies concluded the benzodiazapine family of traquillizers including Halcion that I was taking are capable of triggering major depression. Various studies indicate the illness in its serious stages is not readily treatable or alleviated so, for example, anti- depressants don"t work well without "Talking therapies " alongside and they don"t work immediately in any event! My own chats with the Psychiatrist– not extensive - didn"t seem to help at all. He just didn"t seem to comprehend the nature and depth of the anguish I was undergoing, and perhaps this is understandable. It seems to me they fumble at your head like a "Teenager tugging at a Bra strap" and in the end just maintain their stubborn allegiance to pharmaceuticals of dubious value.

I"m getting ever more desperate. I try some Hypnotherapy and that does fuck all to help either. Mornings are really bad- getting up in the morning almost impossible. Social life virtually non- existent by now. Periods of near- paralysis . Dragging myself to work. Not good. Who the fuck do I turn to now?

In its major stages, depression clearly possesses no quick remedy. Certainly not a "couple of pills and a quick lie down" as many people believe. The disease remains a bit of a mystery, even to those whose certificates say they can cure it. It is a disorder of mood so mysterious it verges on being beyond description unless you have experienced it. William James in his book "The Varieties of Religious spirit " tried to describe adequately the feelings as:

"A positive and active anguish, a sort of psychological neuralgia wholly unknown to normal life."

A feeling of helplessness where one of the worst aspects is the inability to SLEEP , and a sense of constant tiredness never before experienced, accompanied by low self esteem, low mood, and loss of interest in normal activities.

To sleep perchance to dream . No dreams. No relief.

So far as I"m concerned, life had been islands of bliss in a Sea of occasional ennui, where we wander from place to place, to some degree at least at the effect of life"s currents. I had been fairly happy and content since marrying 7 years before, albeit feeling a little "trapped " inside the institution, but I then started to have what I saw as irreversible marriage problems and had split up from my wife and moved to London to work the previous Autumn. The "Seven year Itch"? I had gone back to London to create a new company in the UK for a very large and important East Coast USA Bank in Boston, Massachusetts, and it was a tough assignment. Everything was on the line. It was a big deal, and I needed all my faculties, but my mind was now on my personal problems, with which I was becoming completely obsessed. I had been fine in myself for over a year down in London albeit missing everybody back home, the company was going well, and the divorce was proceeding until, quite unexpectedly, I suddenly started to think perhaps I"d made a big mistake. Should I call it off and go back? Would she have me back? There was the children to think of, which had been making me really sad all year whenever I thought about it. Every time I went back home to see them, I cried when I left. In some ways it would have been better not to go and sometimes I didn"t for that reason.

I found myself caught in the midst of indecision. It was this indecision that eventually did for me , as I then started obsessing about whether or not I had done the right thing by separating.This worry had lead to the sleeping problems and the deepening depression that followed on.

" Come on, snap out of it " , my friends and wife said, when I did go back up to the North to see them and the Kids.

."Sorry " I said, " I can"t seem to do it ". It"s not as simple as that I can assure you. Clearly the pain of a serious Depression is unimaginable to those who have not suffered, and it kills in many cases because the sheer anguish cannot be tolerated any longer. But I had made my bed and I was having to lie in it, however painful that was.

It got to the stage where I didn"t want to go out and when I did, I was just awful company. The phone stops ringing. The invitations stop coming .Somehow I was still keeping going at work, but I had to drag myself there everyday. Drink- my usual comforter- seemed to make me feel worse.Like looking down a long dark tunnel after only a couple.

So drink was abandoned amidst the feeling that it may be part of, if not all of, the problem– it wasn"t, in fact - leading to staying in more, a further reduction in my already poor social life and contributing to a downward spiral. I couldn"t watch TV or concentrate enough to read. Food became increasingly unimportant and without savour. A serious loss of weight followed. I now looked and felt really ill. A sense of anxiety, panic, exhaustion, and hopelessness were my almost constant companions. Exhaustion combined with sleeplessness is a rare torture. My moods were dismal. Days went past when all I was achieving was staring at the walls and obsessing about my problems. I couldn"t bear to see other people enjoying themselves, not even on TV. Because I seemed unable to interact with anyone anymore, I became more and more isolated and lonely which, of course, then makes it all so much worse. I"m okay with my own company for periods, but dislike being alone for too long. But in this new situation, when I was with people, I was bad company and self absorbed so I would get away as soon as I could.

I felt a A change of strategy was called for, and at one point in the proceedings, I went home and discussed it all with my about to be ex - wife, Jean, and practically begged for us to get back together. She reluctantly agreed to this course of action and so, a few months later, they all came down to London to live, which disrupted their lives again. But it just wasn"t working for me for some reason I can"t fully explain and I swiftly sent them back up north again even though the house they had lived in up there, quite happily as it happens, was now sold. So they had to move in with my Mother-in–Law. I shudder to think of it, and the enormous problems this created for them which I have regretted ever since, and for which I will never fully forgive myself. Looking back, I was obviously right in the middle of my "Breakdown" and just wasn"t thinking clearly at all. After this unfortunate episode, I just went right downhill. It was the indecision that finally tore me apart. I just didn"t know what to do.

On top of everything, the particular pills I was taking at that time clearly weren"t working and, as it eventually became clear, they came with side effects. By this time my irrational mind convinced me I was going MAD– whatever that is - and so I began to consider what would happen if I did go completely Mad? Would I just become some sort of vegetable unable to look after himself and confined to an Institution? Sometimes such a disturbed mind will turn to violent thoughts concerning others. Luckily, my thoughts only turned inwards, thus becoming a danger only to myself. The subject of death came into my thoughts on an increasingly regular basis.The thought that oblivion may be good.

Time to "Quit this mortal coil " before it was too late? This is when, unbelievably, suicide started to become an option. Get out whilst the going"s good and I am able to do something for myself, I thought at the time. Thoughts turned uninvited to "Ways and Means "of ending it all. The "Planning stage ". Not ME surely? Stop, wait, think! This is madness. Its an illusion. Isn"t it? This isn"t ME.

Ironically, amidst all this, and a year and a half into the most difficult project of my life, the new company was doing very well, but in the end the situation overcame me - I was losing my family and I couldn"t cope with it. I was in the grip of something that I just couldn"t overcome. Then, I just had a complete breakdown I was powerless to stop.It was overwhelming me …and I could, for now, do nothing to control it and so I tried to run away.

The illness, as it all too often does, had taken a whole new turn.

For the time being I was " Fucking far from being OK ".

CHAPTER TWO
RUMMAGING AROUND IN THE PAST

"Flowers grow out of dark moments"
                                        Chinese proverb

"Childhood is measured out by sounds and smells and sights before the dark hour of reason grows"
                                        John Betjeman

I am English, confident, sometimes seen as arrogant even . I possess, for the most part, an apparently assured manner– at least that"s how many people like to see me. But arrogant people do not usually care so much, as I do, what people think about them. Aloof yes, sometimes, assured perhaps at times, but surely not arrogant? Perhaps the casual observer is mistaken? Au contraire, a little shyness usually well hidden, occasionally a loss of confidence and self belief. I want to be liked. My belief is that those who find me rude merely cannot understand my sense of humour.

Appearances can be deceptive in life.

I believe I am a free spirit at my " core", so commitment doesn"t come easily to me– I like to keep my options open. I"m one of the boys– I like to see what"s out there and around the corner. I can"t help it. For this reason alone, marriage made me feel trapped, particularly in the early years. A lot of married men will be able to relate to this. Yet I have been married for 36 years or so to the same person. At least this was the case until recently!

I didn"t hate my Father or my Mother. Nobody beat me up or raped me or locked me in a cellar for 20 years. I didn"t wear glasses and I didn"t have ginger hair or freckles– unlike the boy from my school on my train every day who did, and to my regret on looking back, I always gave him a hard time- so I did not receive an abnormal amount of piss-taking. As it happens, neither of my Parents were particularly "Tactile"– many parents weren"t in those days, particularly in the case of fathers who were often extremely remote figures - so I didn"t get much in the way of " Hugs and Kisses ".

I now know I"m not a "Depressive" as such, nor have I ever had much to be depressed about over my lifetime. I was relatively privileged in a number of ways, popular enough amongst my Peers and living my life in an increasingly safe and prosperous Land as you will see.

The world I was born into in the late 1940s in Camberwell, South London, was a world without television or central heating– my bedroom was bloody cold in winter, I can remember that! It was a world of vinyl records, rationing and no "Rock and Roll" as yet. But it seemed a happy and now optimistic world nevertheless, having now come out of a war scenario. Community spirit, it seems to me looking back, was much stronger in those days. People knew the other people in their street. The kids played outdoors with each other more.People left their doors unlocked and no one took advantage.People cared about each other.

That these were more law-abiding times than now is not a nostalgic fantasy. The fundamental fact was that, following a sharp upward spike in the post-war years, crime declined markedly during the first half of the Fifties. The numbers started to move up from 1955, but were strikingly low before that time. Notifiable offences recorded by the police were a little over half a million in 1957. Forty years later, they were almost 4.5 million. Violent crimes against the person numbered under 11,000 in 1957, and 250,000 in 1997. It was, in short, a different world.

To me these shocking statistics are a direct result of falling parental discipline over many years and the same at most state schools where Teachers have their hands tied behind their back. Too many kids don"t know where the "line " is anymore. Actually, in those distant days, few people disagreed with corporal punishment in schools. A poll in

1952 found that nine out of ten teachers wanted it retained. Oddly, the victims agreed - in a survey, schoolboys were just as unanimously in favour. It was swift and brief in its execution, whereas alternative punishments, such as withdrawing privileges, were seen as generating greater resentment.

As I say, it seems people helped each other more in those days- and were less reliant on a smaller State - and somehow seemed happier even though not so well off in so many ways as we are today where, ironically, depression is taking a greater and greater hold. Perhaps this is what Prime Minister Cameron is on about when he talks of the "Big Society"– do more for yourselves and don"t rely so much on us.

It was a world where the "Workhouse " still existed and limited Social security was only just being invented, so there was no state pension and social security payments "safety Net" for the poor– now out of control - with people too reliant on it in my opinion. Charles Dickens" "Oliver Twist " was sent to a Workhouse. As it happened, one of my uncles– I had several– worked in a Workhouse as an Assistant to the Overseer.

Under the Poor Law systems of England and Wales, Scotland and Ireland, a "Workhouse " was a government sponsored place where people who were unable to support themselves could go to live and work. It was very much a last resort for people, and many committed suicide rather than go there. Conditions were tough and undesirable– the government did not want to make them an easy option for people. There exists some written evidence that workhouses existed from the early 17th century onwards. My research indicates Camberwell became a Poor Law Parish on 28 October 1835, overseen by an elected Board of Guardians and comprising one parish only, that of Saint Giles. The workhouse buildings on Havil Street had been constructed in 1818. This later became Saint Giles Hospital- our local hospital. Workhouse conditions were deliberately harsh to "deter the able-bodied idle poor from relying on them". Men and women were segregated and children were separated from their parents, often attending special schools called "Poor Schools ". By entering a workhouse, paupers were deemed to have forfeited responsibility for their children. Education was provided, but pauper children were often forcibly apprenticed without the permission or knowledge of their parents. Inmates gave up their own clothes and wore a uniform. There were many well-meaning measures, such as education for children and the provision of doctors and chaplains. However, most Workhouses were run on a low budget, and in many ways the treatment in them was little different from that in a prison, leaving many inmates feeling that they were being punished for the crime of poverty. The terrible conditions in some of them led to depression for many. There were references to Workhouse women who would not speak and children who refused to play. Some Workhouse Masters embezzled the money intended for blankets, food and other important items for their own personal use. Visitors reported rooms full of sick or elderly inmates with threadbare blankets and the windows wide open to the freezing weather. Work was provided to keep the inmates busy. It was usually boring, hard and degrading. Examples included crushing bones, stone breaking and picking oakum. Cooking and cleaning in the workhouse kept many busy and inmates were free to leave but most didn"t have anywhere else to go. How sad.

My, how times have changed!

I was luckier– born into what we would now call a " Lower middleclass family" and never knew a "Workhouse " existed, let alone have to enter one in case you had just started to feel sorry for me! I was born into a period of increasing prosperity and change. One of the most exciting periods of the twentieth, or any other, century was about to start. I was one of the so called "Baby Boomers"–"BBs". Children spawned during that glut of sexual activity that Servicemen returning from the second world war indulged in that led to a " spike " in the offspring graph in the 1945- 50 post war rationing period. Sex was obviously one of the only things that wasn"t rationed, though I never could actually imagine MY parents having sex at all. They never seemed to be the type, although there probably isn"t a "Type". Maybe it was all done in "Laboratory conditions " and they both wore surgical gloves. "BBs " in the UK are now the dominant demographic and were the generation for whom pop radio was invented, music becoming one expression of their generational identity. The "BB" Generation have had a Lucky period so far in their lives, as I will demonstrate later in the book, but will probably get the blame from the generations following them for the present state of the economy and our finances. They are now retiring in large numbers but can we afford the resulting pensions? Has enough been paid in? The feeling is the answer to this question is " Probably not "! In general, " BBs" are associated with a rejection of traditional values.They tend (ed) to think of themselves as a special generation, very different from those that had come before. In the 1960s, as the relatively large numbers of young people became teenagers and young adults, they, and those around them, created a very specific rhetoric around the change they were bringing about and seemed aware of it. As a group, they became the healthiest, and wealthiest generation to that time, and have grown up genuinely expecting the world to improve with time. Lets face it, they have also contributed massively to that improvement, if that is indeed what it is! More on this theme later.

MY EARLY LIFE

I know little of my ancestry, but there is a "Sumner" who was one of the Mutineers of "Bounty " fame. He was captured, with others, on Tahiti in august 1791 by the crew of HM Ship "Pandora" which was despatched to find them and bring them to justice. The ship subsequently foundered on the " Great Barrier Reef " and Sumner and others were lost. I feel this man was an ancestor of mine!

Dad George - a lovely man, very quiet and considered in his approach- served in World War 2 in the REME (Royal Electrical and Mechanical Engineers), and rose to the rank of "Warrant Officer 1", equivalent of a Company Sergeant Major. He served in India and Burma which couldn"t have been very pleasant, and he never talked about it perhaps for that reason. He apparently had a good but "Unremarkable " War during which I don"t think he ever lifted a rifle in anger. He was, after all, not an infantryman, but, as the regiment"s name makes clear, an engineer.

It was the most widespread war in history, with over 100 million military personnel mobilized. The major participants placed their entire economic, industrial, and scientific capabilities at the service of the war effort. The War was marked by significant events involving the mass death of civilians, including the Holocaust against the Jews and the only example of nuclear weapons being used in a war scenario, over Hiroshima and Nagasaki, Japan, which brought a swift end to the war in the Pacific in 1946. Hitler did not invent the pogrom (persecution) of the Jews, but took it to a whole new level.The War resulted in 50 million to 70 million fatalities all told world wide.

Good one to miss, eh? Lucky us.

The war began on 1 September 1939, with the invasion of Poland by Germany, followed by declarations of war on Hitler"s Germany by The British Empire(as it was then), The Commonwealth and France . Germany had clearly set out to establish a large empire in Europe. From late 1939 to early 1941, Germany conquered or subdued much of continental Europe and the nominally neutral (at that time, though this would soon change) Soviet Union took the opportunity to fully or partially occupy and annex the territories of its six European neighbors which eventually became the foundation stone of the USSR. Perversely, In 1941, Hitler"s Armies and their Allies launched an invasion of the Soviet Union, which turned out to be highly distracting and ultimately unsuccessful, particularly given the difficulties Hitler"s armies were to encounter in the cold and snowbound conditions they found in the Russian winter. They were eventually forced to retreat in some disarray, but not until several million soldiers and civilians were dead. In December 1941, Hitler"s ally Japan opportunistically, and unwisely as it turned out, invaded the USA at Pearl Harbor, Hawaii, partially destroying the American Navy, effectively forcing the USA to join the War, which they had previously assiduously avoided. This was much to the delight of Winston Churchill and Free France who had realized the contribution USA were likely to make to the war effort, but had failed to persuade them in up to this point. Unsurprisingly, given the resources of the Americans, this foolhardy act by Japan heralded the beginning of the end for Herr Hitler, as the might of America, combined with Great Britain and the Allied Forces eventually overwhelmed his overstretched armies following the D - Day landings which commenced June 1944 and heralded the beginning of the end of the War.

The War had dislocated ordinary life in a way that had been unimaginable in the happy years of the 30s. Of all the changes that the end of the war would bring, the return of the Men in 1945 was the greatest. A quarter of a million men had been overseas continuously for up to 5 years including my Father. Now, their task done, they would be "De-mobilised ("Demobbed"). But what did they expect to find when they got back? And what of the wives and sometimes children negotiating the occasionally volatile arrival into the house of these virtual strangers? Cosy reunions were often difficult to maintain. Deprived of love, many wives had had affairs, sometimes with tragic consequences, and others had remarried believing their husbands to be dead. Returning Husbands were often moody or distant– some no doubt suffering from some unidentified "syndrome " or other, but most just unused to the home life they had left behind all those years before and missing the companionship of their mates - and so would constantly escape to the Pub leaving wives as lonely as they had been when they were away. There was a more than 10 fold increase in divorce petitions. One wife, made pregnant by an Italian POW, was stabbed to death by her disgusted returning husband. He served a remarkably small sentence of 5 years for manslaughter.

To what extent my own parents experienced these problems is unknown to me, but at least us children were born after Dad got back. Following a great sadness for my parents when my elder sister Annie died tragically after only a few months of life in 1946, I was born by Caesarean Section in February 1947, in the midst of one of the worst winters on record. In the same year the British rule in India– The Raj- came to an end. To give my birth another context, in 1948, the Jewish nation unilaterally created the State of Israel in Palestine, which had been opposed by the British Government as it did not take into account the wishes of the displaced indigenous Arab Palestinians whom they had previously undertaken to protect. The British had been given a mandate to oversee Palestine after the First World War and the subsequent break- up of the old Ottoman empire. The Jews were now pouring into Palestine from all over Europe following the Holocaust, a mass migration which was opposed by the British. Apparently "God " had promised Palestine to the Jews in the "Scriptures" and this is still their profound belief. This put the British in direct conflict with the fledgling Jewish Nation and there was much terrorist activity on the part of the Jews. The British had favoured separate Arab/ Israeli States, plans for which were actually drawn up, but could not be agreed upon by all concerned. What a pity. In the end the British made a hurried withdrawal from the region. As we know, there have been problems in that part of the Middle East ever since, with the indigenous Palestinians being largely displaced and therefore coming off far the worst. Read Leon Uris excellent book "Exodus" if you would like to learn more about the creation of Israel, and the problems caused. Problems which persist to this day.

1947 was also the year the USA launched the "Marshall Plan " which was a very important intervention for a post war Europe that was struggling on the verge of starvation, disintegration and collapse. Who knows, but for this timely intervention in support of western European capitalist democracies, we may have subsided into a USSR controlled Communist satellite. A major irony given we had just saved ourselves- with America"s help - from the Fascist Hitler. Proof, if proof were needed- and I wish this wasn"t so but it is - how important USA is to us. That said, Americans don"t really understand "Abroad " in my opinion, and this has lead to many subsequent misguided forays onto foreign soil, firstly as a buttress against the spread of communism, and then as the "World Policeman". For example, there was Nicaragua , when, during Ronald Reagans Presidency, it is alleged the CIA funded the "Contras " Rebels operations against Noriega"s regime using money raised by running drugs into the USA. Later the phony "wars against terror" in Iraq and Afghanistan to name but two other misadventures. Remember Oliver North who took the rap? America, in my opinion, cannot be completely trusted to do the right thing.

To me, my Parents always seemed "Middle aged ", Dad going bald at a fairly early point in his life. He was a quiet and gentle man. Small in stature and large in generosity. His family came from the grungy sounding Penge, near Beckenham. A Crystal Palace Football supporter but not a particularly serious one. He took me sometimes when I was a kid. I loved Soccer then but a transfer to a rugby only school later in life changed all that. Dad went out to work and Mum (Ivy) looked after us. I never had to do any housework at all, it was just not expected, and I am lazy in this area even now. She was a good Mum albeit not particularly tactile and wouldn"t take any nonsense. She never had a job beyond the home which was what was expected in those far off days- and always had some form of charity work on the go. Her pet project was the Lepers in Kenya where an old English friend was a Doctor at a leper colony. She sold African ebony carvings made by the lepers, and sent the money over to him. A very great and ongoing act of charity which continued for many years. Later she was very big in Youth Club Leadership- whatever happened to those? There were very few houses with two incomes coming in in the 40s, 50s and even 60s. Women became , by and large, housewives once married.

We lived in a typical Camberwell ,South London, Terrace. Next door to Peckham, but posher, if that"s not an oxymoron. Part of the London Borough of Southwark. It gets a mention in the Doomsday Book in 1086 so its been around a while. We lived in Crofton road. Just off Peckham Road and close to the famous Old Kent Road. Worth £60 in Monopoly money (a game that fascinated us from about the age of 11 -Invented in about 1960) and possibly overpriced at that. In our day, trams still ran through Peckham and Camberwell from Blackheath on their way to Vauxhall. By 1952 they had been removed. In retrospect that seems a mistake, since Metropolitan authorities are nowadays building "Metro Rail systems " as fast as they can manage it. The home of the 19th century"s John Ruskin, acclaimed writer, and Poet Robert Browning, so " Cambrewelle" had seen better days to say the least, but it does have its pleasant parts even now. Going west you arrive in a stones throw at the Oval Cricket ground with its famous Gas Holders. Going East, Millwall football ground near New Cross is about the same distance the other way. 2.5 miles from Charing cross.Luckily, I never became a Millwall football supporter, nor even ever went to the ground where they play. In earlier centuries "Cambrewelle" was known for its "Rural tranquillity " and for the healing properties of its natural springs - not any more! Dulwich- rather posher- is just down the road and was where I was born. In East Dulwich hospital. Our house wasn"t very posh at all. "Three up, Two down". Just up the road, our main shopping centre in Rye lane Peckham, where Jones and Higgins store was south London"s best at the time and had my first "Father Xmas" (now closed). Peckham"s landscape suffered from those hideous High rise flats that did the job of housing post-war south londoners, but have been an increasing eyesore and hotbed of drug crime and violence ever since. They can now best be described as "Shitholes" but Peckham is officially described as a "Deprived area ", though to be fair Camberwell is a cut or two above Peckham which is right on its doorstep. Walking distance. Ask the late Damiola Taylor"s Dad about Peckham. 10 year old Black Taylor was stabbed to death in 2000 on the same "Sink "

estate in north Peckham where my uncle, aunt and cousins lived back
in the 50s and early 60s! Delboy Trotter also knows it well!

From East Dulwich Hospital , it is alleged that one can just about
hear the sound of the Bells at St Mary Le Bow about 3-4 miles away
to the north, IF the wind is coming from that direction. I feel I"m a
rather unlikely Cockney! Look, I"ll prove it to you:

"Would you Adam and Eve it", BELIEVE IT
"Get up those apples to bed ", Apples and Pears, STAIRS
"I had a butchers through the window " , Butchers Hook, LOOK
"You"re talking Cobblers ",Cobblers Awls, BALLS
"Use your loaf ", Loaf of bread, HEAD
"I smell a raspberry ", Raspberry Tart, FART
"Whistle", Whistle and flute, SUIT
"Cor Blimey "

Told you I was a Cockney. I don"t sound like one. I sound like a
bit of a Toff I suppose, at least by comparison.Neutral accent, "Received
pronunciation" really , so nobody ever believes me when I tell them this!
I shared a bedroom with my Brother and my Sister had the small room
in those days -she"s now a citizen of Denmark and physiotherapist par
excellence with her own business. After qualifying at Guys Hospital,
London, she spent years in Norway and Iceland before settling in
Copenhagen to bring up the unexpected daughter of the son of the
Bishop of Copenhagen with whom she had had a brief affair! Quality!

I am the eldest. We seemed to fight a lot when younger and sadly
that"s all I remember. No, only joking - we did have some good times
as well! My Dad took me to soccer matches at Crystal Palace and, for a
contrast, the Amateur team "Dulwich Hamlet ". Much later, my rather
more hard–working and practical Brother went to Manchester University
and then became a pilot for British Airways .We were so proud of him.
He lost his job a couple of years later when that BA Trident went down
at Heathrow killing all its passengers because a young Pilot pulled the
wrong lever as the plane was climbing. He had done nothing wrong and
wasn"t even on that plane of course - but they sacked a small number
of uninvolved young pilots anyway amidst claims of poor training as
a gesture, including my unfortunate brother. David ended up as an
"Inspector of Airports " inspecting runway lighting etc from the air in

a light aircraft. After that he went into "Health and Safety " and is now a Consultant. I"m glad someone is making money out of this generally unpopular subject! He and I have never been close partly, I suppose, because we have totally different interests and skills, and so have little in common. He"s quite a good bloke actually– practical, intelligent, quiet and sensitive. He and a mate of his used to make and race "Go-Karts " down at Tilbury docks racetrack back in the late sixties.I was in the drivers seat for a while until I crashed it rather badly once or twice and was not invited again! I was also too big and heavy so it had to carry a lot of weight. Small is beautiful in the Kart world!. A very nasty heart attack followed by a stroke slowed him down some years ago and he"s still not fully recovered. There but for the grace of God etc ….

The house had an outside toilet- no REALLY! And an Anderson air raid shelter in the garden. God fearing Mother and religiously sceptic Father. Uncle Jim, another of Dads brothers, was a Diplomat in Southern Rhodesia–now Zimbabwe which I have visited and is a beautiful country - and would be turning in his grave to see what"s happened there in recent times. He was made OBE in 1961 for services to Her Majesty"s Foreign service. I have the medal and the citation is on my study wall. Granddad on my mothers side was a "Compositor" (Printer) on one of the national dailies. The Star I think. Grandma was just a pain in the arse, as I recall. I never knew my paternal Grandfather. All in all a strikingly eclectic mix of relatives, but I"ve never been a great one for relatives and have never really kept in touch since. As for me, in those days I believed in God because that"s what I was told to do and I had no issue with that. Church and bible classes Sundays. We were clear about our place and discipline was quite tough.

"Children should be seen and not heard " was the mantra. What a terrible thing to say to a kid. However, it was all part of our lives and we accepted it without question. Food was simple and filling – no sign of pasta in our house or any other non- Italian house for that matter. Plain English cooking and lots of stodge was the order of the day. Steak and kidney pie and pudding, sausages and chips, beans on toast, Mums famous " Sumner special" was a regular feature on the menu (Mash, bacon, grated cheese) smoked haddock, tripe, welsh rarebit, spam and chips- spam and EVERYTHING. Fish and chips from the shop fridays and always, always roast joints on sundays. We read Noddy books like everyone else of our age.

Meat, butter, cheese, sugar and sweets were still rationed in 1953, and blitzed inner cities remained, even if many of their inhabitants had been shipped out to suburbs and new towns. War films were the staple diet of the cinema -The Dam Busters, The Cruel Sea, Reach For The Sky. War was central in children"s lives and imaginations. Airfix Spitfires, sold by Woolworths for two shillings, proved to be the toy firm"s most popular model, while boys" comics were full of stories of "Braddock, Ace Pilot", "Sergeant Allen of the Fighting 15th" and "The Eyes that Never Closed" about hunting German U-boats.

Here are some other examples of what our lives were like which I came across on the Internet the other day (unattributed and I have paraphrased and added things of my own). If you are about my age they will bring back some memories:

"My favorite fast food when I was young? We didn"t have fast food. Everything was slow.

Where did we eat then? A place called Home! My mother cooked everyday when Dad got home from work. Oh, and we sat round the dining table! If I didn"t like what was on my plate, I was made to sit there until I did like it. You didn"t leave the table without permission in those days!

Here are some other things about my childhood years:

My parents never wore jeans, owned their own house, traveled out of the country or had a credit card. With the exception of the house, if they couldn"t afford to buy it cash, they never bought it. They never went to posh restaurants until much later in life and they never drove me to school. We had to walk or go by train or bus on our own. Teachers and Prefects could cane us at my school. We were never the worse for it either–it engendered good discipline so lacking in schools today where Teachers have so little sanction.

I never had a phone in my room and my parents had a "party line " with people down the street. You had to make sure no one was using it before you did so.

Most newspapers were delivered by boys and most boys delivered newspapers. I did, and it was the hardest work for the lowest pay I ever did. Up at 6 am and off I went before school for years and if I was ill, my Mum did them so as not to let the shop down!!

We played "marbles" and "Jacks" and collected "Cigarette cards " of famous footballers, cricketers and so on.

Movie stars kissed with their mouths shut and there were no profanities and explicit sex scenes.

How about the following:

Using hand signals in the car to turn.

Trouser leg clips for Bike-riders.

Sweet Cigarettes.

Deliveries to your home of milk and fizzy drinks–"Corona".

Pathe News reels. TV test patterns.Peashooters .Blue disposable flashbulbs.Cork popguns.Washtub Ringers."

Things aren"t what they used to be, are they!? My, how things have moved on!!

The West Indians began to move into our area straight off the SS "WindRush", that famous Immigrant ship that brought many of them over in the 40s. At that time their were no restrictions on allowing citizens of the British Empire from moving to the UK. The steamship docked in Tilbury 22 June 1948. It had stopped in Jamaica to pick up some of the thousands of Caribbean servicemen who had been recruited to serve in the armed forces during the second world war. They were joined on their Atlantic voyage by some 500 other Caribbean men and women wishing to visit England. They were housed temporarily in shelters in Clapham, south west London near, unsurprisingly, Brixton, which was to become the main centre for them in the years to come. Many did not intend to stay, but over the years "The Windrush generation" and their families have become integral to our society and began our change to the multi-cultural society we see today, although they were by no means the earliest immigrants to these shores.

For example, there was a limited flow of people– often crews from ships docking here who then settled -mainly from the Dominions around the time of the first world war, and some Chinese, who were treated with great suspicion, and any English girl who took up with one was treated like a bit of a leper!

We can, of course, go back to the Romans, the Vikings, the Normans and the Angles, Saxons and Jutes (from Germany) the Gypsies and the Jews when talking "Immigration" but I will leave it at that!

The following story was told to me by my Grandmother, Nan Dohoo (a rather unusual name, the origins of which I have yet to discover),when I was quite a lot older:

" One day, when I was about 4, I was walking down the street with my Nan and a Black Man -an early immigrant- stopped to pat me on the head and, rather charmingly in retrospect, said to Nan what a beautiful child I was. I asked why he had a "Dirty Face "? Whoops! "

Of course, I had no concept of "Blacks" in those days. None of us did. They were, in fairness, very new to our shores, in numbers anyway. Luckily, he was okay about it– actually laughed. Anyway there was as yet no Race relations Board in those far off days. Nan went Bonkers in the end. When she died, in our house where mum had been looking after her, we found many of the drawers in her own house full of Brown paper bags– the type you used to be given by shopkeepers to take your purchases home- that she had saved. Bio-degradable of course, way ahead of their time. What on earth she thought she was going to do with them all, God only knows.

In those years , my Parents had a most ingenious, and regularly employed, modus for controlling us when we were overly naughty. They used to ring "Mr Simpson". " Mr Simpson" was, as it turned out, the entirely invented owner of a "Home " for naughty children. A picture of the deprivation and punishment to be experienced there did not need repeating. When we got out of control, Mother would ring him - pretend to ring him as it happens. But she always had a finger on the button of the phone so no call was actually made. She would explain the problem in our earshot, and instruct him to come and pick us up forthwith! We of course were always distraught at this turn of events, and through our tears, promised, PROMISED, we would be good … PROMISE, PROMISE!!!

The frightening "Mr Simpson", of course, never did make an appearance which we never seemed to notice. Was this cruel? I don"t know, but it worked! We never used the method on our own kids though!

In 1950 the first Credit card system was introduced and the mass production of "Mainframe "Computers began, not that I was aware of it at that time.

We didn"t have a Television in our house until I was six in 1953- they were just hitting the market. It was so tiny in its little wooden box. It was, of course, black and white and about 9" across. One of the first. I still remember us all sitting down for the Coronation of Queen Elizabeth 2 that same year which got the TV revolution well and truly under way. No one wanted to miss it of course so those that could afford it bought one! How excited we were.We all got coronation mugs. And little Flags. The station went off air about 10 pm, after playing the national anthem -when did that stop - and back on the air at about 6 am. One station only of course! " Muffin the Mule " and "The Flower pot Men " early recollections. Later it would be "Dixon Of Dock Green". The BBC - slow-moving, highly bureaucratic and with no appetite for taking risks or giving offence , was the embodiment of respectability. "I want you to see yourself as an Officer in a rather good Regiment," was how Robin Day was welcomed to the "Radio Talks" department in 1954. News bulletins remained pillars of grammatical rectitude and only "Received pronunciation " allowed.

New Zealander Edmund Hillary and Sherpa Tensing conquered Everest in Coronation year 1953 and I played the Angel Gabriel in the Primary school play. The Star of the Nativity. That same year my brother hit me over the head with a garden rake in an argument. There was a lot of blood! I imagine lots of people, especially my wife, would have done the same since if they"d thought of it. "Uncle Dick ", a friend of my dad who lived down the road was a "Commercial traveller " selling stationery products (now called salesmen). We used to holiday in Broadstairs, Kent, with them and their kids, and he might just as well have been a real Uncle as our families were so close. Dad and he eventually had a big fallout– we never found out what it was about - but we avoided them from that time on. One of my real uncles, Ron, was a bit of a rough diamond compared to my Dad who spoke "Received pronunciation" as did we. Ron spoke with a true South London accent. They hardly seemed brothers as Dad went to a grammar school in Greenwich through his own efforts and learnt how to talk " proper ". Ron went to the Secondary modern so kept his "Sarth Lundon " accent, but was now making a fortune selling printing ink. Much more than my Dad who had a " respectable " , and excellent, Accountancy job with Shell Oil, for which company he ended up working loyally and faithfully for no less than 50 years at which point he got the Gold Watch! Sales was not regarded as "respectable " in those days. One of Dad"s Brothers -in - law, my uncle, had a pig farm down Folkestone way. I developed a love of pigs on my occasional sojourn at the Farm helping out in school holidays. He was a hopeless businessman as it happens - especially careless with money in spite of Dad"s good advice which he ignored- and they were always fairly badly off. It was difficult sometimes telling whether one was in the farmhouse or one of the Pigsties! I know Dad gave them money to help from time to time, which was typical of him.

The backdrop to all this was the austerity of fifties post war England. Our parents had just come out of the nightmare that was the second world war remember, and were just grateful there were no bombs dropping on them anymore, and nor were their sons and husbands and loved ones being killed. By the 50s the "Cold war" with the USSR was in full swing. The Korean war–started 1950, ended 1953 - was the USA lead war against the spread of world communism part 1, part 2 being Vietnam in the 60s. Mercifully it was supported by relatively few British troops. More on these wars later.

England, the favourites, were beaten in a shock defeat by USA in the 1950 Football World Cup, so were eliminated.

As the Peckham area was becoming distinctly Caribbean by 1954, and anyway Dad was doing well at work– he was now a Chief Accountant at Shell Oil International– we moved out into the Shires. To Kent. First to Shortlands near Bromley for a year or so until the house developed dry rot, then, temporarily, to Southborough near Tonbridge Wells into a tiny little House that had been no more than the "Lodge keepers " house at the gate to a large old estate.We had a wood between our little house and the school about ½ mile long which we had to walk through on our own . The school was 1 mile away. Mum just sent us up the hill. We were only six years old. For me, this wood was far too like a forbidding wood that featured in one of Enid Blyton"s Noddy Books. "Noddy"s Wood" we called it, and we were scared stiff everyday we walked through it, especially in the dark winter evenings. We would never be expected to walk alone in such circumstances these days. Even so, you wouldn"t ever regard my mother as uncaring - it was just how it was in those days. As I got older the Books would be Blytons "Secret 7" and "Famous 5" . Then, even later, Arthur Ransome"s, to me, spell-binding "Swallows and Amazons ".Books about a group of young friends and sailors set on and around a Lake district lake. Daniel Defoe"s "Robinson Crusoe" a bit later caught the imagination. Beano, Dandy and later on, Eagle comics were regular fare. I loved all of them. Like everyone else, we got Chicken Pox. Do as many kids still get this? I remember the smell of wet clothes on a wood frame in front of the coal fire like it was yesterday. About this time - I was seven I think—I started to learn the violin. Apparently I was quite good and got to grade 5 by the time I was 11 or 12. I nearly got a scholarship to Winchester School as a result at 11. Of course, when I eventually went to the City of London school (see later) I used to get the piss taken regarding my violin case. I nevertheless persisted with it for some years and even was asked to play to the class and join the school orchestra. Sadly as all too often with kids, I gave it up at 15 when I should have been developing it, distracted by sport and other interests. Shame but typical.

The 60s decade of the dawn of the great youth revolution and its new music culture was still a few years away, and even Elvis was in the future , in 1956, when his "Heart was broken in a hotel " somewhere! The Teddy boys, with their "Drape " Jackets and big "Duck"s Arse" hairstyles came and went. The Jive endured, though few are adept at it these days—well, apart from me and the Missus that is. We can still do a good turn around the Dance Floor!

"You show me yours and I will show you mine", I said to the 6 year old next door. I was seven and unimpressed with what I saw, although she seemed quite interested,   but of course neither of us knew what was supposed to happen next.

We moved to suburban Orpington, Kent, in 1955 when I was eight, and set up Home in one of those three -bedroomed 50s Build Middle Class Estates. I went to Crofton Primary School, then Crofton Juniors. The same name as the street where we were born- just a strange co-incidence! To get to it we had to walk a mile or so down by the side of the Orpington to London Railway line-again on our own often as not.

No 4x4 Mums in those days. Mum just sent us off with our backpacks and sandwiches. The famous "Golden Arrow " Pullman steam train was a regular sight as it sped to the south coast on a daily basis, and I admit to being a keen "Trainspotter" in those far off days.

One time I remember deciding to leave home I was so upset with my parents strictures. I must have been all of eight. So I put my pet caterpillar in a matchbox and marched off down our road resolving never to return. Of course, when I got to the end of the street , I didn"t have a clue as to where to go, and, after standing there for ages, wandered back with my tail between my legs!

I was a good "Wolf Cub" and would finish up with an armful of badges, but my later transfer to the Boy scouts was less successful as there was an attempt (unsuccessful) to interfere with me at my first camp and so I never went again. At about the age of ten, I do remember playing "Ratty " in our school"s musical version of "Wind in the Willows". Ratty is a very good part. 2nd Lead. I was very good apparently, even though I was physically sick with fear and the resultant sore throat meant that I could hardly sing any more. I was, of course, more interested in sport and was Captain of the Soccer 11 and the Cricket 11. I was good at them both. I loved sport but, crucially, I was lazy academically which would cost me dear later. One or two of the girls used to chase me in the school playground but every time there was only one winner–CW - who went on to play women"s cricket for England. She was the fastest girl in the school by some distance, but regrettably NOT the best looking , and definitely NOT the one I fancied!

The first Queens speech went out on the television in 1957, about this time.

Certainly the Junior School years, by and large, passed uneventfully, apart from when the great Manchester United Team of the late 50"s– The Busby Babes -went down in a snow bound airport in Munich in 1958. Tommy Taylor, Duncan Edwards,Roger Byrne, Dennis Viollet and some other football Stars , along with a few "MU" staff and journalists including Frank Swift, retired legendary Manchester City Goalkeeper, all dead. It decimated the team, but a week after the event, two of the surviving players and 9 of the second team went out and beat Sheffield Wednesday in a league game. Unbelievable. Football Fans the world over grieved. At least Bobby Charlton was spared along with Harry Gregg, goalkeeper and Bill Foulkes, with whom I once played golf. I, and several hundred thousand others around the world became "ManU" fans at that very point. In my case lifelong. To this day, most MU fans are located outside of the Manchester area and in that sense "MU "are a unique football club. I now live in the Manchester area, had season tickets for many years,now surrendered, but occasionally am invited into the Directors Box with old friend and now Life President Martin Edwards so there! That said, I must say I"m not entirely happy with the way football has gone generally in the last 20 years or so. The high wages and player behaviour my two main problems.

Buddy Holly was the new singing sensation about this time, and we had our own little skiffle band at school. I was on the "comb " covered by tissue which improvised as a musical instrument, I seem to remember! Then there was the incident that, I believe, made me terrified of standing up in public and speaking for years to come. A phobia I eventually, to my credit, managed to overcome, but not until I was well into my twenties. Our Teacher in the last year at primary set us a task to get a hobby– I chose Astronomy for some reason. I did do a bit of work on it but was bored and left it.Then one day in class months later, he raised the subject of Hobbies out of the blue, and wanting to see what we had achieved , unfortunately picked on me to tell the class about astronomy! Well, to say I was unprepared is an understatement! I was ten at the time.

"Stand up Sumner " he said.

I did so but, having nothing to say as I didn"t know anything, I just stood there with my mouth open. Inevitably he ridiculed me in front of the whole class who all fell about laughing. Needless to say, no one else was made to get up and that was that. I was left feeling a pratt. It was only after having to do work presentations and Best man speeches (frightening) much later in life that I regained my confidence! Well these little incidents shape us and make us what we are I guess.

I then managed to fail my 11 plus.That I was going to pass was a given, but I didn"t and everyone, Teachers included, were genuinely shocked. As it turns out subsequently I"ve never been particularly good at exams due mainly to lack of application, but I had been expected to pass this one. In mitigation I was unwell that day . So, as a result, I was now headed for the local Secondary Modern School. That is until Dad "s deepening pockets intervened- we were getting much better off as he was doing so well at work . Now he WAS a hard worker. Never stopped. He had a long time obsession with The City of London School through an old friend who had attended the school, located in the City , then at Blackfriars Bridge on the River Thames near Fleet street, now relocated at Puddle Dock just down the road. Allegedly, they were a bit choosy about who they took on, so I wasn"t over-optimistic about my chances. To my surprise, and probably everyone else"s, I did well and passed the entrance exam– not so "Thick " after all then! Dad was over the Moon. I was just relieved!

The school was founded in 1834 and is ultimately governed by the City of London Corporation headed by the Lord Mayor of London. School Alumni include HH Asquith, Prime Minister at the turn of the 20th Century, Kingsley Amis, the Celebrated late Author , and Daniel Radcliffe (Harry Potter). In my time there we had Sir Peter Levene, ex - Lord mayor of London and Whitehall Grandee. A really good bloke who I had the pleasure of sitting next to at an Old Boys Dinner sometime in the 90s, and Mike Brearley,whose father Horace taught us Maths, an intelligent and successful cricketer who went on to Cambridge to study Classics and Captained England cricket with some considerable success in the 70 s and 80s and went on to be President of the MCC not so long ago. Academically brilliant, and a fantastic Captain, he even tamed Beefy Botham and, according to Botham in his autobiography, was the "Best Captain I played under ". My friend, ex -England cricketer Paul Allott who also played under "Brears", agrees. Praise indeed as these Guys- now cricket commentators on Sky- don"t do praise very often! Brearley"s Book "The Art Of Captaincy " is worth a read for any budding Leader of Men, sporting or otherwise. He went on to be President of the MCC many years later and is a regular contributor to "The Times" newspaper. 2009 fees were £12,267 per annum. In my first year they were about £100 per annum! The City Of London was a very good School, and a very academic school.Oh dear!Sadly, I turned out to be not hugely academic. Not a "swot ", lets just say that! Completely the wrong school for me- perhaps somewhere like Millfield with its emphasis on sports would have been more appropriate -, but no doubt rather better than the alternative with which I had been faced only months earlier. "Secondary Moderns "sounded so depressing. Anyway, I was chuffed and so was Dad about my getting into this illustrious Institution, but it meant a daily rail commute from Kent into London. Quite a pain actually and the train was usually overcrowded. I often had to stand up, which was not good since I often had homework to finish (or even start!) The journey door to door was about one hour. I always got up at the last possible moment , but had perfected what needed to be done to get me out within 10 minutes for the seven minute walk/ run to the station to catch my train, and I rarely missed it - the 7.45am Orpington to Blackfriars. Sometimes I even had a valid season ticket, and sometimes I spent the money Dad gave me for it on something else– sweets probably- so had to duck and dive round the Ticket Inspector, sticking behind the crowds as much as possible and flashing the out of date ticket as fleetingly as I could without arousing suspicion. Miraculously, I never got caught.

We always had to give up our seats on the train to ladies of whatever age, and even for the older geezers– stuffed shirts plodding to the "City " for the umpteenth year. Dead from the neck up, and just going through the motions most of them. I resolved never to become like them, and, apart from fleetingly, never have. Mind you, they may have been more conservative than today"s lot, but at least the Bankers seemed to know what they were doing in those days, and their pay was conservative and proportional.

We gathered in the school"s magnificent Great Hall for prayers and hymns every morning at 8.45 am(late arrival always got you a detention) and our Class took delight, whenever it was "To be a pilgrim ", in singing loudly and anagrammatically ".Grimple " instead which, for some reason, always amused us hugely, silly little boys that we were . We played Football in the playground most lunch times with a tennis ball and in the Summer would play cricket with the same ball using a waste paper bin as the "Wicket ". Ricky Nelson was singing "Hello Mary Lou ", Brian Hyland " Here comes summer" (bastardised by friends to "Here comes SUMNER" for obvious reasons), Johnny Tillotson was singing "Poetry in Motion"….., Gerry and The Pacemakers were singing "I like it" …Bobby Darin "Dream Lover"...Bobby Vee "Like a Rubber ball"... Paul Anka "Diana". …favourites all. Some of the Teachers just couldn"t keep control of us, so with them we never learnt much. The school had its own indoor swimming pool.By all accounts our Swimming Master was "Queer", although, whilst I personally was never approached, one or two of the boys reported being "Touched", but he was never grassed up so far as I know. We all had to swim and dive in the school pool in the nude– a nice parade for the alleged paedophile several times a day! A bit tough on our ever growing "Knackers ", not that mine were growing nearly enough for my liking. "Chopper" Bill had the biggest Knob and we were all jealous- still are. The Swimming Master seemed to pay particular attention to Bill- bit of a "Teachers pet". Bill was also the class "Bully " in those days (since reformed!) Funny how these things work out, as he and I became great friends many years later. I caught "Sinusitis " one day after a swimming match when I had to sit around the pool all afternoon with no tracksuit on freezing to death waiting for my next event. I have spent the next 50 years having various degrees of respiratory problems with my sinuses. Eventually I had an operation on them which gave me some relief over time.

I remember the whole School had to do an annual 3 mile cross country run which I, and many of my class mates, hated with a vengeance. I played wicket keeper and No. 5 Bat in the school cricket team and flanker in the rugby team– No:7. I couldn"t wait for sports periods but for the field sports -Rugby and Cricket - we had to go to Grove Park, South London, on a train. About an hour away all in all which was very inconvenient indeed, and not conducive to after school practise in the evenings enjoyed by most of the other schools on our fixture list.

We all joined the "CCF"- the Combined Cadet Force " which had the three Service "Arms", Navy, Army, Air force, where we played "Soldiers and Sailors ". I was in all three at one time or another.We went on a minesweeper once and I was sick and later were taken up in various aircraft including a chipmunk doing aerobatics- I was sick again! In the army section we would spend hours crawling round Richmond park on our stomachs playing soldiers although there was occasionally light relief shooting 303 rifles at Bisley Range which was, of course, great fun.

The Lord Mayor of London (whose show we annually took part in) and some celebrity or other– I remember actress Dame Edith Evans made quite an impression on us one year- gave away the prizes at Prize day. One year I sang Handel"s Messiah with the school choir in front of a packed school hall. At this time my classical music side was being suppressed in favour of more "manly " pursuits, but it was surprisingly good fun.

About this time, to give it a time context, Chubby Checker had just invented the "Twist ", a new dance craze that meant we danced apart from our female partners for the first time ever. It was certainly easier than the Waltz or the Foxtrot, in which we had been dutifully schooled. It seemed very strange at first–not like a dance at all - but it caught on big time, and many variations have followed on since. Apparently it was derived from an african /american plantation dance called " Wringin and Twistin", which can be traced to the 1890"s and has its roots in Africa. I had by now progressed to reading the Eagle comic–Dan Dare and the Mikon. My Dad had bought an Austin 7 and soon after an Austin A30- a tiny little car which somehow fitted the five of us in for day trips to the Kent Coast.

Anyway, back to school. I was in the fourth stream (out of five) so I was not a top scholar, but, in my defence, it was a very academic school with lots of exceptionally bright pupils. I was usually in the top three to be fair. Class VD, in our " O " level year, were a nightmare group of pupils– always messing about in class, and really taking nothing seriously.

I can"t remember which class was our "Wanking " class , but in this 5th year, French was our smoking lesson. The teacher, one "Rocky" Cornish, was so lax some of us always smoked at the back of the class. He never said anything so we assumed he hadn"t noticed. That is until towards the end of term just before we were due to take our "O" Levels. He made an announcement:

"The following Boys will fail their French. Sumner, Jones, Garland, Smith …" etc.About seven of us.

" The reason is you have been smoking in my class and not paying attention. The rest of you will pass".

We were gob- smacked. So he HAD noticed, just didn"t say anything. No detentions, nothing! What an odd man and such a weak and rubbish teacher. But he was a great bloke and ran our school holiday trips for years. In one trip, to Germany, he arranged a wine tasting and we all drank far too much, ending up being "sick as dogs" and sleeping it off for the rest of the day. I couldn"t drink Riesling (or any white) wine for many years after that experience ! We were only 15, so I"m not sure Rocky had exercised the requisite amount of "Duty of Care" in this situation. However, in many ways he was a gentle man and like a father figure to us, but he was much too soft in class. In the event, and utterly ironically, I was the only one in class to actually pass French, largely due to the fact I had spent 2 weeks that Easter in Le Havre with a french pen pal which had really got my French oral going (I got 95% in the oral exam!) I eventually did french "A" Level at night school and still get by on french as this next story rather subtly demonstrates:

Many years later I went into a french restaurant and asked for "Le crème d"Ouefs ". (Egg Custard)

The waiter said, very pompously,

"Its not " LE Crème d"Ouefs ", its "LA" Crème d" Ouefs– Its feminine ".

I said,

"Its not FEMININE is it ? Its CREAMED EGG! What do I need to know the sex of an egg custard for? I want to EAT it, not FUCK it"!

My classmates all the way up to the end of the 5th year were all crackers and, as I say, did too little work. Consequently, we collectively made a bit of a mess of our exams with various consequences . The consequence for me was I didn"t get enough passes to go straight into the 6th form, so had to waste a year in a kind of " mezzanine " level class doing more O levels. At the end of that year, we treated all our teachers to a special lunch in the canteen by way of apology for the way we had let them, and ourselves, down.

Notable boys in the class (who were actually the two maddest amongst us) but went onto good things were Hugh "Spew " Jones who became a Colonel in the British Army, David Turner who founded the LA Fitness chain and made a lot of shekels (he was my only Jewish friend),and D.M. "Dim " Robinson, who went on to become a pilot with BA, the youngest Captain they ever had – and later on was invited to join the Concorde programme. What an honour that must have been! The next year in the Junior 6th form, and split up from most of my mates into the science sixth, I seemed to turn into a "Flashman" type of character for a while and gratuitously beat up an upper sixth former–ironically the school orchestra"s lead violinist Danks, alongside whom I could easily have been playing violin had I so chosen - for annoying me in some way and not for the first time. They had to treat him for cystitis as he was such an irritating cunt. This particular time, I think he tried to give me a detention for a minor misdemeanour or something and I had had enough. But he was easy prey and I much regretted it afterwards, particularly as Danks subsequently reported me and so I was summoned to see our rather frightening Headmaster, Dr A.W. Barton, a bit of a legend and very hot on discipline. I was made to stand outside his office in some trepidation for some time before I was called. The Head boy was in attendance and he made it clear I was going to be suspended at the very least.

"Come in " sounded like the crack of thunder to me. The Head was standing at the huge fireplace in his imposing victorian study, hands behind his back, swaying as he talked, face like a Turk at a Christening. Just how I imagined "Tom Brown schooldays " Dr Arnold to be. Luckily, I got off with a serious caution and detentions, but "bottom line ", I was lucky not to be suspended.

All in all, I was never an academic success, partly because, in retrospect, along with most of my classmates, I really never worked hard enough and university held no appeal as you will discover later.

Holidays with the family in these years were usually taken at Folkestone, Poole, Bournemouth or on the Jurassic coast of Dorset at Swanage, Lulworth Cove, Old Harry Rocks, Chesil Beach, Corfe Castle, Thomas Hardy"s Dorchester, and day trips down to Weymouth were all on the agenda. It has delighted me that, in recent times due to son Adam now living in Poole, we have been able to re-visit these places that mean so much to me from my childhood.

Almost nobody had credit cards yet and the culture was still, by and large, not a credit one. My dad was very clear about it.

" Neither a borrower nor a Lender be son " he told me firmly.

As a Banker and mortgage and credit card holder later in life, I became both as it happens!! So much for parental guidance, in my case at least.

Controversial "Kitchen sink "dramas on TV depicting homelessness, backstreet abortions, sex and four letter words were changing the face of television and enlightening us as to what was going on in our world. This was reality TV, 1960s style.

In 1961 when I was 14, Russia"s Yuri Gagarin made the first orbit of the earth in a spacecraft to the annoyance of the Americans- who then started to play catch-up in the "space race "with a vengeance which would eventually lead to them achieving the first "Man on the Moon". In the same year a revolution was about to occur in British comedy, although I didn"t become aware of it until several years after the event, being too young. It was at the Fortune Theatre in London"s West End. The show, an "Anti–establishment Review ", was called " Beyond the Fringe ", which had premiered in the Edinburgh Festival the previous year, and starred four people who went on to become legends. I refer of course to Peter Cook, Dudley Moore, Alan Bennett and Jonathan Miller. Oxbridge luminaries all, who had created one of the most original shows to hit the stage. Ahead of its time, unapologetic and surreal, it included the famous "Tarzan " sketch, " One leg too few ". This featured Dudley Moore as the one legged man auditioning for the (film) part of Tarzan.

" Mr Spiggott, when you came in I couldn"t help noticing, almost at once, that you are a one-legged person, a Unidexter"

and

" Am I to understand that you, a one legged man, are auditioning for the part of Tarzan? This, a part that normally requires a minimum of two legs."

" Your right leg, I like. I"ve got nothing against your right leg Mr Spiggott.The trouble is, neither have you!"

All this according to Peter Cook"s character, the film"s Producer. Another sketch lampooned the War:

Squadron Leader (Cook) to Flight Officer Perkins:
"I want you to lay down your life, Perkins."
"Right sir!"

"We need a futile gesture at this stage. It will raise the whole tone of the war."

"Yessir!"

"Get up in a crate, Perkins."

"Sah!"

"Pop over to Bremen."

"Yessir!"

"Take a shufti."

"Right sir!"

"And don"t come back."

"Yessir"

"Goodbye, Perkins. God, I wish I was going too."

"Goodbye Sah!– Or is it au revoir?"

"No, Perkins, (it"s goodbye)."

Hilarious and ground breaking! Inspired by this new form of comedy– "Satire "- came shows like "That was The Week that Was " with David Frost et al, "Monty Python ", "At Last the 1948 show ", and "Private Eye" Magazine owned then by Peter Cook – a must read for many of us in the 60s and 70s. Years later "Not the nine o clock news ",with a rampant Rowan Atkinson and Pamela Stephenson (Mrs Billy Connolly), memorably carrying on the tradition.

While on the subject, no book written by me would be complete without at least a mention of Peter Cook and Dudley Moore"s outrageous characters "Derek and Clive", invented by them in the early 70s.Drunken alter egos in conversation, full of swear words not originally intended for public consumption, but a bootleg copy got out somehow and became a smash hit underground, so they just got on and released "Derek and Clive Live " in 1976. I bought a copy straightaway and have laughed with it ever since, particularly with my mate big Paul. Memorable moments from the records include Clive claiming that the worst job he ever had was " Retrieving lobsters from Jayne Mansfield"s bum". (a metaphor for Crabs I guess?!)

Derek"s worst job was "cleaning up Winston Churchill"s bogeys ", concluding the Titanic was one such bogey,albeit a very large one, and it "went to sea, the fucker sank and the band played on".

We can only admire their straightforward point of view. Poets?

Satirists? Philosophers? Comedians? Social commentators? Derek and Clive sum it up more succinctly. "Just a couple of cunts" is their frank self-appraisal."

But to continue:

In 1962 the much loved Marilyn Munroe died of an overdose of Barbiturates, at least that"s what the record books show. Some believe she was actually assassinated by the American Secret Service, as it was perceived she had become a liability to the Country due to her affairs with the Kennedys and her subsequent indiscretions. In other words she knew too much. A student of the famous New York "Actors studio" and a contemporary there of Marlon Brando, she had been the lover of both Bobby and John F Kennedy, and, by reputation, the lover of anyone else that would appear to love her. Hers is a sad story of success, loneliness and depression.."Goodbye Norma Jeane." The final years of Monroe"s life were marked by illness, personal problems, and a reputation for being unreliable and difficult to work with and, riven with doubt and self loathing, feeling unloved and unfulfilled, she appears to have taken her own life. The official verdict was "probable suicide". How very sad. As it happens, my personal favourite film of all time is " Some Like it Hot " in which she stars with Tony Curtis, doing a fantastic Cary Grant impression, and Jack Lemmon. My other top three films are Schindler"s List and The Godfather.

At about this time- I was fifteen or so - I tried my first cigarette. I bought a packet of "Gold Leaf ", went to the local woods one Sunday afternoon, and, full of guilt and great expectation, lit up. It didn"t go well. My body couldn"t take the filthy whirl of smoke and I coughed and never stopped. My ears buzzed and I felt very sick. My body was trying to tell me something about this alien substance. I should have listened. I spent all afternoon in bed. For some reason, this experience didn"t put me off! It would have been better if it had.

Feminism started gaining a hold at the beginning of the 60s and Feminists were taking to the streets like the Suffragettes before them. Here was the beginning of the end of the world in which women suffered in an all too misogynistic world where they created domestic bliss for men by being tied to the kitchen sink and tending to the children, from whom the Fathers were frighteningly aloof and distant in those days. Prior to the 70s women"s place was regarded as being in the home.For many, it was a life of empty pointlessness from which, too late, they could not escape. Women were actually excluded from many jobs and professions and left to concentrate on bringing up the family. By and large women were remaining chaste until their wedding day before the 60s although there were, of course, exceptions to this rule. This was about to change, and women were soon to be presented with a new and powerful tool to help them make their own life choices. The contraceptive pill , having come to market in 1961 for married women only, was made feely available to girls and women in 1970. It was to change their lives forever and put THEM in the driving seat for the first time when it came to decisions about when to have a baby, but also helped lead to the sexual free for all that was to come. The pill, developed by American biologist Dr Gregory Pincus, works by suppressing ovulation, and was initially tested on, presumably disposable, Haitian and Puerto Rican women. Previously, many pregnant girls and their lovers had been forced by their parents into unwanted marriages. For the women who still got pregnant in spite of the Pill, this all changed with legalised abortion. Additionally, women now started to get jobs in previously male dominated arenas. Feminism was on the march. Women were breaking out. Women were also now far more inclined to say "yes" to a shag as it was safe to do so. Sex was no longer the big risk it had been. By the mid -seventies, men and women were having sex with anyone they fancied as a result. Sex was fun and recreational. Homosexuality was legalised with the "Sexual offences act " of 1967, to which I have no objection, but I personally hope it never becomes compulsory! Divorce was also on the increase- people now disinclined to stay in loveless marriages just for the sake of it. It seems to me women, whatever they may think, have made great progress in their war on prejudice against them.

"You"ve never had it so good " Harold Macmillan, Prime minister, had said in 1963, during a boom period for the economy, which turned out to be another false dawn. Macmillan"s career had just about survived after being lampooned by Cook in "Beyond the Fringe "whilst sitting in the audience one night but didn"t survive the notorious Christine Keeler affair that engulfed his Government in 1963. One of his Ministers, John

Profumo, had been introduced to this nymphet and Escort / prostitute by a so- called society osteopath, one Stephen Ward, who had also introduced her to an alleged Russian spy, Yevgeny Ivanov. The security implications were serious and, when this all became public, Macmillan"s government wobbled and was eventually to fall the following year in the general election of 1964. The dread Socialists were back after an absence of many years. Let the spending begin as usual with them. Ward was charged with living off the earnings of a prostitute, and committed suicide soon after.

In 1963 Valentina Tereshkova, another Russian, became the first woman in space, and the Americans became even crosser. The Great Train Robbers stole £20m and some of them went to jail. Biggs escaped and spent the next 40 years in Brazil! I went out to work in that same year having had, by then, more than enough of school and no ambition to go to University. I went to work in Insurance in the "City " because an older acquaintance somehow managed to make it sound glamorous— it is not!

Deference still ran deep in British society - whether towards traditional institutions, senior people in hierarchical organisations, prominent local figures such as Teachers, Bank Managers, GPs, older people generally or the better educated, and the epitomy of this was to be found in the City of London. In the ultra-hierarchical "City", it was still "Mr this" and "Mr that" in most offices. I was " Mr Sumner" and my Boss was "Mr Clifford ". I recall many, many employees going to work in bowler hat, short black jacket and striped trousers, but not me thank goodness!

Meanwhile, Elvis was having "Fun in Acapulco ", his latest film, this one with the glamorous Ursula Andress.

THE SWINGING 60S

So, in 1964, Harold Wilson became the first Labour Prime Minister for some 16 years. I was at the Sun life Insurance Society, Cheapside, in London"s City, right opposite Mary Le Bow church. Now there"s a coincidence.

The phenomenon that was The Beatles were by now in full swing and had changed everything in the music world.We waited in great expectation and speculation for their new albums to come out . They arrived in 1964 in America to be greeted by 10,000 delirious fans, appeared on the Ed Sullivan TV show, and became the most famous band in the English speaking world virtually overnight. Just like that. The "Swinging sixties "had indeed started .

And so sang those legendary Liverpudlians from the "Cavern ":

"Do you love me "? - Yes we do!

"Can"t buy me love " - True!

"All you need is love "- well, not quite all perhaps.

"Its been a hard days night" - If you"re lucky.

"Eight days a week "- Only if you"re God.

"We can work it out " -. Ode to marriage ?

"I want to hold your Hand "- we used to change the last word for "Gland" and fall about laughing like silly little Boys (which is what we were). Still are.

"Eleanor Rigby " - Who she?

But its certainly been a "Long and winding Road " for me, that"s for sure.

Now I"m a "Paperback Writer "– Pulp fiction, more likely.

Some idiots later demolished the original "Cavern" so, eventually needed as a tourist attraction, it was rebuilt on the other side of the road!

Our Dansette record player was well used I can tell you! A new age was about to dawn– in retrospect one of the most change in history. The Youth of England were about to break out.

In 1965 The Hippie movement started in San Francisco and Timothy Leary was "Busted " for carrying marijuana and later experimented with LSD which I never went anywhere near. The Mamas and Papas were "California Dreamin", Donovan was being a "Universal Soldier", and the Animals "Gotta Get out of this Place"....... The Yardbirds, Georgie Fame,and the Blue Flames, The Who were smashing up hotel rooms and guitars as they went - the heroes of the Quadraphenia set -and the Rolling stones followed on and, like the Beatles, ruled the airwaves. The Yardbirds were singing "Over under sideways Down". Radio ships Caroline and London were out there in the North sea off the Frinton coast in 1965 defying broadcasting regulations . Pink Floyd was founded that very same year-one of my favourite bands of all time. The original Moody Blues had already been founded– in 1964, but was yet to become famous. "On the Threshold of a Dream ", my favourite Moodies album, was not born until 1969. That same year a man stepped on the moon for the first time. The fabulous Queen band was yet to materialise. Formed 1971, "Killer Queen " was the song that first made me conscious of the bands existence.

1964 was a memorable year. As I said, I was now out at work, having decided academic life was not for me at the age of 17. I had amassed a miserable haul of 6 "O" Levels and my Dad was furious, not surprisingly, as I had left school without mentioning it to him! Whoops! Trying to find my "Niche ", I tried job after job, but nothing seemed interesting. I was yet to become the driven and moderately successful businessman that appeared somewhere during my mid to late twenties. Nevertheless, it was all good experience. Anyway, I passed my driving test that year and the "old man" bought me a motor. He had promised to do so if I would forgo motorcycling at the age of 16! Not, it has to be said, any old motor.Nothing less than a motoring classic - an MG TC sports circa 1947. I nearly killed myself several times, was always drinking and driving like everyone else and got pulled up for speeding and all sorts (but never for drinking and driving), so much so my Father eventually determined the car had to go for something a little safer. A Minivan was a bit of a comedown but hey, it got me around. I drove down all the way to the south of france in that car to our holiday villa in Cap D"Antibes the next year. Drove all night!

Sometime around 1966 we went out to the Radio Ships - London and Caroline - in my school mate Gingers speedboat which was kept at his parents Frinton holiday home in Essex. We spent the weekend there, most of us sleeping on the floor. The ships were anchored up just outside the 3 mile limit off the coast in the North Sea to get around UK broadcasting restrictions and had become our default radio stations- an integral part of the burgeoning 60s youth culture - the stuffy BBC having failed to recognise and pander to the pent up demand amongst youth to hear continual pop music on the radio. A crowd of us, girls and boys, visited both ships that day in Ginger"s boat and, to our excitement, met several famous DJs of the time who came on deck to greet us. From memory, Johnnie Walker, Dave lee Travis, John Peel, Tony Blackburn and one or two others.

"Smashy and Nicey "! Fab!

But things then started to take a turn for the worse. As it happened, our engine conked out and we were cast adrift—subsequently found to be due to a lack of oil in the petrol! Typical Ginger, and more of him later. He had spent all day on the saturday servicing the engine, keeping us all hanging around, then forgot the oil! Seeing us drifting, Radio Caroline put out an "SOS" for us and a sailing yacht under power came to the rescue and towed us back. Oh the shame of it!! That weekend me and Paul were in my motor.By now, through shortage of funds, I had been forced to downgrade yet again to a very dodgy Standard 10 with a bashed in passenger door that pre-existed my ownership of the car, which I couldn"t afford to have mended.On the long way home to Orpington , suddenly there"s what looks suspiciously like a fight going on in the middle of the Mile End road, East London, not the nicest part of the Town, at 2 am Sunday night, and right in front of us. As it so happened, we had just been trying to figure out how to make 2 miles worth of petrol last the 10 miles to Herne Hill where Paul lived - neither of us had any money as usual- then fate took a hand. We stop. It turns out to be a Policeman struggling with a "Tea-leaf" who had been robbing a nearby store, and in the middle of the road for goodness sake! But not a moments hesitation on our part. I jump out and help the cop. Paul rings the cop station for reinforcements. The burglar is tamed and our reward? £3 in old money for petrol - enough to get us home and more - from a grateful Peeler, and a letter of thanks from the Commissioner at New Scotland Yard! How "bout that? Doesn"t seem likely does it, but it"s a true story! You couldn"t make it up! These days you would give the whole thing a wide berth. What a lark. And what an eventful weekend.

The "swinging sixties " were now in full swing. The beginning of the generation whose obsession with the pursuit of material possessions was to become the defining characteristic of modernity culminating in the 80s hysteria. The 60s was of course the era of many new things, now the stuff of legend. It was a very special era. It was our era. It was the perfect antidote to those austere post war years we grew up in, although our parents were, with some justification, mildly suspicious of what was going on. Youth was taking over is what was happening. We were re-inventing the world. We were inventing Sex (at least we thought we were) but talking about it a lot more than we were actually doing it, although to be fair many of us were actually doing it, at least to some extent. There"s never enough is there? Fashion had changed dramatically– Mary Quant, BIBA, mini skirts, Carnaby Street boutiques, denim jeans.There has never since been a period quite like it.

Amidst all this there was a real music revolution going on. Apart from the Beatles and the "Stones ", the Yardbirds were my favourite in those years, with their particular brand of Blues based Rock and guitar pyrotechnics. As I will demonstrate, they became highly pivotal in that they played a key role in the development of several other great bands that followed on. We were great fans, and went to several live "Gigs ".

Fostered by the Kingston Arts school where their original members were students, "For your love ", recorded 1965, is still one of my all time favourites. The London Marquee club in Wardour street was our usual haunt, and the Yardbirds were regulars there long before they became nationally known. In the Original Yardbirds Band was Lead Singer Keith Relf, who died of electrocution at his home in 1976, Samwell–Smith, co- founders Chris Dreja and Mc Carty and Top Topham, who was replaced in 1963 by Eric Clapton. The other Yardbird legend, Jimmy Page, joined later in 1966. Page eventually left to form the "New Yardbirds "which ultimately morphed into–yes, you"ve guessed it. " Led Zeppelin", a band that was to gain its own place in music history. Clapton himself went off to join "Johnie Mayall"s Bluesbreakers " in the late 60s, then co-founded "Cream" with Ginger Baker and Jack Bruce, and was replaced by another now legend, Jeff Beck who was later fired, in 1966, for missing shows allegedly due to illness. The "Yardbirds" unhappily split in 1968 just before the first Isle of Wight Music Festival -that"s over 40 years ago! Beck went on to form the "Jeff Beck Group", yet another great Band. Keith Relf and Jim Mc Carty formed, in 1969, what was to become "Renaissance".

So you can now see just how important "Yardbirds "was in the history of Rock!!

The great Clapton himself was elevated to the " Music Hall of Fame " no less than three times.

Q. Can you remember what for?

A.Once for "Yardbirds", once for "Cream" and once as himself! How good is that!?

We would usually venture through the heart of Soho on the way home from Wardour Street. China town close by. Leicester square around the corner. Wonderful pubs, delicatessens, cafes, restaurants, speciality food shops, Theatre land all around us, and the Strip clubs of course. These visits were always tinged with some excitement for other reasons, imagining what lurked behind doors with postcards marked "Come inside for Lulu–sexy brunette " or "I"m Crystal- come up and knock 1st floor ", but we never went up to find out, preferring the relative comfort -zone of the strip clubs.

We used to go and see great Jazzman Georgie Fame at the" Marquee " and at the "Ricky Tick "club down Surrey way. Fantastic he was. Big Fans." I say Yeh, Yeh ....and in the evening..".

Rhythm and blues icons Manfred Mann"s band formed 1962 was another favourite, who I originally saw at our local village hall in Orpington in the early 60s as they were starting out. I also seem to remember seeing Screaming Lord Sutch, Gene Vincent, and the Rolling Stones in their (very) early days at the same venue! The iconic and ground breaking Rolling Stones first made their appearance in 1962 and were an instant hit with their particular brand of Rhythm and Blues music grounded in black american music culture and inspired by the likes of Muddy waters, BB King, Chuck Berry and Mose Allison. The "Stones " actually came from round our way–Sidcup and Chislehurst. As the 60s marched on, they became the epitome of "Swinging London" and the new drug culture that went with it. Their haggard faces nowadays tell their own story of the dissipated life they have lead for the last 45 years. Real Rock Groupies we were with our Burtons hand made blue serge suits and Modern "Beatle Cut " hairstyles. At other times, though not "Mods" as such, we wore the "Mods " default Uniform– Levi jeans, Polo shirt, Hush puppy suede shoes, but because of our backgrounds we were not typical "Mods" in any way at all. The Mod and Rocker riots in Brighton Hastings and Clacton were just around the corner in 1964. We were there too, obviously more "Mod " than "Rocker " even though my Mate Rick had a Motor Bike rather than a scooter– a 650 BSA "Beezer" and I was on the pillion. I was 17. We often took purple hearts- " uppers "- Phenobarbitone (Drinamyl, an amphetamine) which gave us a high of sorts which we didn"t really need. I haven"t touched drugs since. Well, perhaps the odd "Spliff" but never got anywhere near "Coke ". We were hangers on really- not at the centre of the action at all but it was all great Fun! In fact the " Riots" were nothing more than a bunch of kids running around making a lot of noise, squaring up to each other and breaking a few windows. Of course, as is their wont, the Press had a Field day the following Mondays after these events, but the truth is, it was all rather harmless. Of course they "Bigged Up" to make the story interesting as usual. The film "Quadraphenia" tells the story rather neatly " though Sting over a cliff on a scooter in the final scenes was a bit over the top. We called the Girls "Sorts " in those days– God knows why. With their "honeycomb" hairstyles, mini skirts and so on. I can picture them now and my girlfriends at the time were usually dressed thus. As many normal Monday nights as we could me, Dave and Ricky would go to the legendary Mecca Ballroom in Purley– a huge Barn of a place called "The Orchid",where Diana Ross and the Supremes were in full swing with "Baby Love ", Mary Wells sang about "My Guy", and Ike and Tina Turner were thrashing out "River deep and Mountain High". We saw them all "Live ". The place was always jumping. We did pull Birds on a regular basis of course and I would shove mine in the MG, always with a few pints down me I"m ashamed to say, and take her off down a quiet lane nearby…and I was beginning to sample the delights of older, sometimes married women who were continuing my sexual education.. Marvellous. Friend Dave– he was from Purley and sported an expensive and much sought after full length maroon leather coat which were " De Rigueur " dress at the time - was a real rogue. Bit of a "Mod ". Always on "Pot". Bit of a "Tealeaf" too, albeit a public school one. When he was at school, he used to forge his season ticket expiry date– he was well organised that"s for sure - a and never got caught. He was always nicking things, and one "Job" was breaking into a nearby Rugby Clubhouse to steal Fags and drink. Apparently this was a well known and vulnerable target locally. One time, I sat in the car waiting for him. Technically I was his accomplice. Our fathers would have been quite horrified! I shudder to think of it, even now. Anyway, we got away with it thank goodness, and with me he never actually stole anything– the Rugby Club were getting fed up with being robbed and had installed better security. I heard the new burglar alarm go off, and 2 minutes later Dave was sitting beside me in the car panting:

"Lets Go"!!

and we sped off. I often wonder what happened to him in the end though. Probably something bad. He was a head-case. We all used to go to Brighton at other times before and after the riots and sleep under the famous pier, staying out all night at Brighton"s night clubs and getting high on "Purple Hearts ". Searching desperately for the "Free Love" everyone else seemed to be getting in abundance! Stealing milk off peoples doorsteps for breakfast.

I was leaving religious practise, though not yet belief, behind. My choirboy days were becoming a thing of the past–yes that"s right- where I had been a boy soprano soloist of some note and latterly a Bass / Tenor. They ended with my friend Jackie W"s unexpected and early marriage in 1965. She was the only reason I had stayed so long. Sexiest choir girl, or girl of any category in my view, in the district, of whom my Mother definitely did not approve. She turned out to be a bit of a "Goer " as they say, and this came across to my suspicious Mum who proceeded to hamper our relationship as much as she could. More about Jackie later. I also left the "Crusaders" Bible group at the same time, of which I had been a member since I left the Boy scouts at the age of twelve due to the attempt to molest me at summer camp by one of the Leaders to which I, unsurprisingly, objected as I mentioned before. The "Crusaders" was a Christian youth group founded in 1907 by a man called Albert Kestin. Its now called the " Urban Saints" apparently. It was all good fun for a young Christian, with great camping holidays and its own mores and traditions. I became "Born again" in my time there which must have spanned five years or so. Oh by the way, one of the Crusader Leaders was subsequently successfully prosecuted for molesting one or two of the boys in our group. You can"t trust anyone, can you! See Roman catholic priests and their love and predilection for little boys in the chapter on "Religion".

Anyway, I was branching out. In 1965, at 18 years of age I,

predictably, got fed up with my second boring job, this one in the Uniroyal Company"s Tredaire Carpet Underlay Division as someone"s assistant doormat . This had followed on from the even more boring Insurance job and, along with a colleague from Uniroyal, resolved to change our lives. In my case not for the last time.

CHAPTER THREE
THE WATER SKI INSTRUCTOR

My work Pal at Uniroyal had a mate with a speedboat so we talked. We all needed to "DO something ".

So we went over our options and eventually decided to go to Spain and start a water ski school there. Just like that. I was now 19 and it was 1966. My Dad was less than impressed. His view of life was that if you have a job, you stick to it - that"s what he had done and many like him had done the same. But I was already into my second job after 3 years following school. But the world was changing with less loyalty, and us youngsters were pushing the boundaries.

I"d never been to Spain. Not many people had at that time. Most post war family holidays in the 50s and early 60s were taken in England. We had ours at places like Broadstairs as I said before - sand castles on the beach a fond memory. The cheap package holiday for the mass market was yet to be invented. As it turned out,we could have done with a bit more research and preparation for the Ski school! I could Water ski, but not very well- Ginger had taught me to a basic level in the freezing waters of the North sea near his parent"s Frinton cottage. The Boy with the speedboat was very good though, and he ended up teaching me properly.

We arrived in high spirits in a long since lost Benidorm, in the heart of Dictator General Franco"s Spain. Our Speedboat in tow behind us. Franco"s strong anti–communist regime had emerged in 1936 from his victory in the Spanish civil war. Franco was the BOSS. His word was LAW. His was a police state-The "Guardia Civil" the Instrument of his power - and all opposition was ruthlessly dealt with. When he eventually died in 1975, the monarchy under Juan Carlos was restored, along with a return to democracy.

I digress. In those days Benidorm was a much more pleasant environment that today"s Fish and chip "Grab a Granny " nightmare. It seemed a beautiful place to us then, with its sprawling Bays, its genuine Spanish food, its Bars so different from our English Pubs. It was a pretty Town, a village really, and the multitude of High rise hotels that were soon to invade the skyline to accommodate the package holiday hordes were still to come. It didn"t take us long to discover "San Miguel " Beer and "Cuba Libres ", "Paella" and "Tortilla", and we were up and running . I quickly learnt to do "Mono" and "Beach" starts. Sadly, It wasn"t long before our hopes for the ski school were well and truly dashed. We had very quickly discovered that, to start a ski school, we needed all sorts of permits including a "Residencia" and a permit from the "Commandante Di Marino" which we had no chance of getting, at least not this side of Xmas- it was April! Who had been in charge of research prior to this trip?

"Fail to prepare......prepare to Fail.."

So we did what any red blooded Englishman would do under the circumstances -we went ahead and started the school anyway! Fuck "em. It went really well for a while and, as legend has it, being a Ski Instructor DOES do wonders for ones ability to pull the Birds. It certainly did for mine ....and it wasn"t difficult making sure we "accidentally " knocked girls tops off as we got them back on the boat—ooops so sooory! We were having a great time and sex with the Holidaymakers was (sort of) freely available. It must have been all of 3-4 weeks before we were "Sussed", told to get the boat out of the water, and piss off (Vamos!). It HAD all seemed too good to be true and it was! They were VERY cross- I got the feeling they were doing us a favour by not putting us in Jail! General Franco was the Boss and you don"t Fuck with him. So the Boat owner did " Vamos ", took his boat, and the other fellow went with him. I stayed on alone and got a job with another ski school. Perfect! For now! The next few weeks passed pleasantly until that ski school closed as well and I was out of a job. There was no Bar or other work available so I soon ran out of money and couldn"t afford my rent. I wasn"t eating either. I was, however, drinking courtesy of generous holiday makers. Drinking on an empty stomach wasn"t a good experience of course. A better one was the day I met famous American film actor Jeffrey Hunter and his then girlfriend, the lovely Sally Ann Howes, a well known "English Rose " actress, who took me back to their swanky apartment and very kindly filled me full of food, which was extremely welcome as you can imagine . They had been filming in Madrid.

My Landlord, an unpleasant Chinaman, wasn"t pleased with the rent situation, and confronted me one day outside the Apartments.

"Where is my money you Clunt (SIC) "?

One thing quickly lead to another. I told him to piss off, he would get his money sometime but he wasn"t taking NO for an answer. He took out a wood file or some such object and lunged at me sharp end first! I moved out of the way almost in time, but he wounded me in the side, and blood started to flow! This was getting serious! I somehow got away, and was taken to hospital where I got stitched and bandaged up and filed a complaint against him. I still have the scar to prove it happened and I didn"t dream it! He also reported me to the Guardia Civil. In the end they decided not to press charges against him, but I was told to leave town. No justice but I started it and at least I didn"t have to pay the rent!   I didn"t have any money anyhow, and needed a new job, so I hitched up the coast to Sitges, south of Barcelona, long before it became Spain"s "Gay " capital, and got a job in a new Bar for a while. "Sinatra"s Bar ", so named because we only had one record–Sinatra"s Greatest Hits - which was played "back to back" endlessly! The same Bar pedalled "Beef burgers " made out of Horsemeat! Quite tasty actually, until you found out what they were! I taught water skiing there too and lusted after the Swedish and Dutch Birds that seemed to be were everywhere and readily available. There was this particular Dutch girl I was expecting to shag but, but…I was about to make a somewhat irrational decision.

All in all the Spanish trip had been a mixed, but mainly happy, experience, but all good things come to an end, and, for no particular reason, I felt I should go back home. More fool me.

HOMEWARD BOUND

When I got back I needed a job. Any job. So, lacking imagination as usual, I got job in the Bakery in downtown Orpington where I was back living with our parents !! A place famous for a rare Liberal party by election win (by Eric Lubbock) in the 60s in what was a Tory stronghold, leading to the expression "Orpington man" -a media created new breed of commuter voter who had unexpectedly turned against the Tories who had been in power some 10 years at that point. It wasn"t long before I wished I was back in Spain! I needed work and money fast, so had gone in desperation to the famous Wonderloaf Bakery. On the production line working nights! NIGHTS! Endlessly putting dough in tins, taking bread out of tins, putting bread in ovens and so on.Tedious, relentless boredom. I was lucky- some people were there for life.What a waste of a life. Anyway, 6 months later I"m having recurring nightmares. Same dream over and over - trapped in the oven surrounded by baking tins and can"t get out. When my dad wakes me up, as he had to several times, , I"m standing up in bed HAMMERING at my bedroom walls with my now bruised and cut fists and SHOUTING to be let out. Clearly going barmy. To avoid going completely Bonkers, I had to leave. Ironically, many years later, as a Freeman of the City of London (the side benefit of which is I can,theoretically, drive my sheep over Blackfriars Bridge), I was invited to join a City Livery company.

Trade and craft associations have flourished all over Europe for many centuries, but the City of London companies, now collectively known as the Livery, are unique in their survival, number and diversity. The Livery companies still flourish today as living institutions. Their survival has been achieved by doing what they have always done: fostering their trade in a wide context, serving the community, and embracing modern skills and professions. Today there are 108 livery companies in the City of London and they are ranked according to their status and historical importance. The Mercers (General Merchants) are the most senior, followed by, in order of precedence, Grocers, Drapers, Fishmongers, Goldsmiths and Merchant Taylors. The best ones have their own premises– " Great Halls " and "Club" rooms and so on. Quite by chance it was the " Bakers Company " I was invited to join, which is 19th on the list, so reasonably important. I was interviewed in solemn circumstances by some 10 committee people. They asked me a series of really pompous and annoying questions challenging my fitness to join their precious club and, after about 20 minutes of this, I had had more than enough. Keen to establish my credentials, but no longer keen to join them, I then merely enquired:"Look, gentlemen, have any of you ACTUALLY BAKED a loaf of bread "?

They were clearly astonished at my presumption to ask, but of course none of them had! I explained my credentials– because I HAD worked in a Bakery as we know - made my excuses and left abruptly to the genuine astonishment of all those gathered !

Anyway, back to the plot. I was drifting - I needed to get a serious career started and I needed to escape the dreaded Bakery. I was 19. So I left in desperation and got a job in the "China and glass" department of the (fairly) well known store "Gorringes " in Victoria. Ok it was well known in Victoria, just around the corner from Buckingham Palace! The tedium of this particular job remains indescribable, but there were no more bad dreams and there was some variety as I had an occasional sojourn in the store as a catwalk model for the men"s clothing department. Titter ye not!

Some months later, and dissatisfied, I then got on an underground train, and went to look for a job in the City of London, my alma mater. And that very day I did get a new job , and it was the first job I was offered as it happens, but, quite by a stroke of good fortune, it turned out to be the bottom rung of where I am today. Just a clerk but it was better than baking bread or selling china and glass to non existent customers ! It was in an unimportant City Merchant Bank but was something to build on and build on it I did as you will hear later! I ended up staying 5 years!

It was good to be settled and I was quite enjoying the, rather undemanding at that stage, job. The Rugby season was just starting so I did have a bit of light relief. I played for the Schools "Old Boys "Team. Rugby was soon to become a priority, and I actually turned down a job as a "Cub Reporter " at the Local paper as journalists have to work weekends, and Saturday had become " Rugby day"!

England won the World (Football) Cup that year and that was pretty good, but we didn"t see it as we were training!! The 60s was a great time of fun and innocence, looking for the "Free Love " we had heard about but couldn"t always find! No seat belts and no worries about drinking and driving–the breathalyser hadn"t yet arrived and nobody gave driving with a load of booze on board a second thought. Just as well. We would play the game, drink copious pints of beer then drive all over London half pissed. Everybody did it. Oddly, and luckily, I never had an accident. Never felt incapable. Never got caught, but the Police in those days weren"t really looking for drink drivers anyway. Rugby was my main passion. Cricket also, both of which I played for my old boys teams, The "Old Citizens ". We were having a great time.

We learned to survive it all somehow. At least, most of us did. Some, like two of my best friends, didn"t.

CHAPTER FOUR
SLIDING DOORS

A year or so later, In 1967, with my new career starting to blossom, we all went to Spain for a holiday. For me it was a pilgrimage as much as a holiday. The party was eight old school friends , some from the Rugby club and some other school friends, in 3 cars and we took Ginger"s speedboat. To Denia, on the Costa Dorada near Valencia. We hired a Villa as was our custom in those days. This was the year of the glorious "Sergeant Peppers lonely Hearts club Band" album, allegedly written by Lennon and McCartney whilst high on drugs-"Lucy in the sky with diamonds" was accepted as the clue to the drugs use - the sounds of which formed a constant backdrop for the holiday. Sounds like the work of LSD to me. I think we wore that album out over the two weeks and I even met the lovely Sally who I went out with for some months afterwards once we were back in England. Marvellous! It was all going really well then some local man got killed in a car crash just outside Denia a couple of days before we were due to come home. We heard about this, and me and my mate Paul rather morbidly resolved to inspect the crash site. The scene, a winding mountain road, was deserted, but the car was still there, its bonnet well and truly caved in and its windscreen missing, glass everywhere. The car was a " SEAT 500.", the Spanish version of a Fiat 500, and made in Spain. On the seat, amongst much dried blood, was a really flashy and clearly very expensive camera which we could have just " half–inched ". But we felt we shouldn"t and didn"t out of respect. Why had no-one else taken it? WHY it was still there I can"t say. Typical of the Spanish. I"ll move it "Manana". It was all too weird and we felt funny about it. It would have been like walking over someone"s grave if we had stolen it. But, as it turned out, this event must be regarded as a curious omen for what was to come.

We all set off back to England in high spirits and three separate cars, but unbeknown to us, disaster was just around the corner. Rog and Howard (along with Paul and Ginger, my best and oldest friends at that time) went together in Rogers " Triumph Spitfire " sports car. I went with Paul in the far less exciting "Hillman Imp". The four of us kicked around all the time. Rogers parents ran a boutique hotel in Bayswater and I was always stopping over after nights out on the Town. I can remember seeing Cassius clay knocked down by Henry Cooper on their Television in June 1963. Rog and Howies accident occurred on the notorious N7 two lane highway - crucially short of a central crash barrier - just south of Paris. Hit head on by a lorry. They were both 20 years of age with their whole lives ahead of them. Howie, a Graduate of Oxford University working at BP in the "Britannia House " city tower block that was its home at that time , and Rog starting to be successful in the Property World. Apparently the driver– we never found which of them was driving– accidentally touched a kerb, bounced across the road into the lorry"s path and they were dragged back 100 yards from whence they had come. One of them was thrown out of the car, and landed on his head. The other was forced back against a tree still in the car, the car caught fire, and he was frazzled to death. Our two best mates gone … just like that. What a terrible end to a great holiday. We were about half an hour behind Roger in our car, and, another strange twist, we broke down, never to re-start, also on the N7 south of Paris not far from the accident! If we hadn"t conked out, we would inevitably have come across the crash site, so at least we were spared that, and our breakdown was one hell of a coincidence under the circumstances. We ended up taking a train to Calais then home via the Ferry. The AA brought the car back on a Trailer in the usual way. We thought we had problems! I found out when I got home. My father loved those two boys who he knew really well, and was standing in the kitchen crying his eyes out as I came in. I burst into tears too. We had been virtually inseparable for years.

Now "The twist in the tale ".

As it happens I was supposed to be in that car, but Rog and I had a row just before we left- over Sally I think, who he felt I had pinched off him - and Howie went with him instead. I remember how jealous I was. I needn"t have been. I was just about to experience the biggest slice of luck I have had before or since. I often wonder how things may have been different- would I have been killed or would it maybe not have happened at all. "Sliding Doors"? Their parents never recovered from it. The funeral was such a terribly sad occasion-its always worse when there are young people involved. Parents should never have to experience burying their children. They never get over it. Its on their minds 24/7 I"m told, and I can believe that. I sure hope I never have to experience it. To make it even worse, if that"s possible, the boys were both only children. Their parents spent the next 10 years seeing "Spiritualists " trying to bring them back from the dead. They believed in all that rubbish too. Surely a simple con trick? The three musketeers and D"Artagnan were now the two musketeers. Me and Paul Shippard.. Still going 40 years later and grateful for it. Where was God when all that was going on?

CHAPTER FIVE
ASSASINATIONS, WARS AND MUSIC FESTIVALS

Fairly soon after I was born, the Korean war started between North Korea, supported by Communist USSR and the Peoples Republic of China, and South Korea, supported by 16 United Nations sponsored countries. The USA provided the largest number of participants as usual. The war was a result of the physical division of Korea by an agreement of the victorious Allies at the conclusion of the Pacific war at the end of World War 2 and was about halting the spread of Communism, about which the USA in particular were obsessed. It began in 1950 and ended in 1953, by which time 3 million-mainly civilians - were dead with little gain, other than it did actually keep South Korea out of Communist hands. The Iconic 1970 Feature film "MASH ", concerning one of the first "Mobile Surgical Hospitals " in Korea, whilst a bit of a spoof, depicts the horror of war very well and is well worth the entrance money. Although supplying a relatively small force, Britain lost more troops than in the Falklands, Iraq and Afghanistan put together. The end of the Korean war heralded the start of the so called "Cold War" with the USSR which was escalated in 1961 with the rise of the Berlin Wall which became the focal point of the War.

The 60s turned out, amongst other things of note, to be the decade of some notable assassinations. President Kennedy"s assassination in Dallas in November 1963 was the first. We all remember where we were when we heard. I was in the local cinema with my girlfriend and a message was flashed up on the screen. I"m not sure what the film was-it may have been "Billy Liar "- but nobody stayed to the end. We were so shocked and everybody went into mourning. So young, so great. He had faced down the Ruskies over Cuba, with the help of a Russian Mole in the Politburo feeding back their tactics as it turned out. But what a Naughty Boy– conquests too numerous to record here included Marilyn Monroe. Of course we didn"t know about his secret life in those days- he was just a hero. Conspiracy theories abound, even to this day.There has been speculation that it may have been either the Ruskies or the Mafia that had him killed but it is generally accepted that it wasn"t Lee Harvey Oswald, the accused who, before his trial, was gunned down by one Jack Ruby, a club owner. Mysteriously, some 64 witnesses to Kennedy"s death allegedly died over the next 18 months or so, many in strange circumstances. Co-incidence or something far more sinister? We will not get to the truth now.

In 1968, Martin Luther King was assassinated bringing grief to both sides of a nation and the world. King was an American clergyman, activist, and prominent leader in the African American civil rights movement. He is best known for being an iconic figure in the advancement of Civil rights in the United States and around the world, using non violent methods following the teachings of Mahatma Gandhi. A Baptist minister, King became a civil rights activist early in his career. King"s efforts led to the 1963 March on Washington, where he delivered his iconic "I have a dream " speech of which the following is a memorable extract:

> *"I have a dream that one day this nation will rise up and live out the true meaning of its creed: We hold these truths to be self-evident: that all men are created equal.*
>
> *I have a dream that one day on the red hills of Georgia the sons of former slaves and the sons of former slave owners will be able to sit down together at the table of brotherhood.*
>
> *I have a dream that one day even the state of Mississippi, a state sweltering with the heat of injustice, sweltering with the heat of oppression, will be transformed into an oasis of freedom and justice.*
>
> *I have a dream that my four little children will one day*

*live in a nation where they will not be judged by the color
of their skin but by the content of their character.*

*This is our hope. This is the faith that I go back to the South
with. With this faith we will be able to hew out of the
mountain of despair a stone of hope. With this faith we will
be able to transform the jangling discords of our nation into
a beautiful symphony of brotherhood. With this faith we
will be able to work together, to pray together, to struggle
together, to go to jail together, to stand up for freedom
together, knowing that we will be free one day. And if
America is to be a great nation this must become true.
So let freedom ring from the prodigious hilltops of New
Hampshire. Let freedom ring from the mighty mountains
of New York. Let freedom ring from the heightening
Alleghenies of Pennsylvania!*

I have a Dream today"

And America did become better, but I suspect it still needs more
work in the racial tolerance area !

In 1964, King became the youngest person to receive the Nobel Peace
prize for his work to end racial segregation and discrimination through civil
disobedience and other nonviolent means..

By the late sixties the so called " Flower power " era was in full
swing, and we were all wearing flower patterned shirts, beads " singing
love songs and so on. It was a slogan used by the American counter
culture movement during the late 1960s and early 1970s as a symbol
of passive resistance to the Vietnam war.The expression was coined by
the American Beat Poet Allen Ginsberg in1965 as a means to transform
war protests into peaceful spectacles. Hippies embraced the symbolism
by dressing in clothing with embroidered flowers and vibrant colors,
wearing flowers in their hair, and distributing flowers to the public,
becoming known as "Flower Children " and we all copied in. The term
later became generalized as a modern reference to the hippie movement
and a culture of drugs, psychedelic music, psychedelic art and social
permissiveness (In other words, lots of "Free Love ").

In 1967, we had our first Colour television Channel– even our winning world soccer cup performance in 1966 had been in Black and white!

In 1968 President Johnson signed the Civil Rights act. Civil rights movements in the States were gaining footholds and change was in the air. Then Robert Kennedy, three months into his Presidential campaign, was gunned down and killed by Sirhan Sirhan, a 24 year old Palestinian Immigrant with no apparent axe to grind.Yet again this left a Nation and a world in mourning, in particular the Black population whom Kennedy had famously championed.   Maybe his assassin was an Agent of the Mafia, whom he had determined to eradicate, or the Klu Klux Klan, or maybe Sirhan was aggrieved about the 6 day war with Israel, of which the date the shooting was the first anniversary, but the true reason remains a matter of speculation? The black population of America had lost two Champions in one year and Sirhan is in prison to this day.

Princess Diana"s death in the 90s was the next time The Baby Boomer Generation was to feel so aggrieved.

VIETNAM

Having got going in 1965, by 1968 the Vietnam war was in full swing with no sign of progress– shades of Afghanistan and Iraq 40 years later.Some lessons are never learned-the English army was thrown out of Afghanistan in the 19th century after a disastrous defeat costing the lives of thousands of our soldiers and their Wives and families! In April 1965 there were 25,000 US troops active in Indo China (Vietnam). By 1967, and with hundreds of American soldiers dying every week, there were over 400,000 US troops based there and still not winning. It was a disaster. The 70s film "Deerhunter" starring Meryl Streep and Robert De Niro captures it all magnificently. The war was fought between North Vietnam, supported by its communist neighbours, and South Vietnam, supported by anti-communist nations.This was yet another disastrous conflict attempting to prevent the spread of Communism. It ended with the fall of Saigon in April 1975 after 20 years and effectively defeat for the Americans and their Allies. Some 58,000 US servicemen died or went missing in action in the conflict and, it is estimated, between 1 and 3 million Vietnamese died, many of them civilians.

WOODSTOCK

On July 20th 1969 Apollo 11 lands on the moon and Neil Armstrong walks, the same year as 500,000 partygoers trudge in the mud to Woodstock music festival , in the United States. 200,000 only were expected. Chaos! Woodstock, the most famous Rock n Roll Music festival in History, took place Aug 15-18 1969. I was 22 and becoming an expert in "Invoice Discounting". Beatniks, Hippies, Flower Children and Rock Legends gathered together not in Woodstock as it happens, but in Bethel, rural New York state. The idea came from Band Manager Michael Lang and Artie Cornfeld, a record company executive, who wanted to raise money to build a Recording studio in Woodstock where there was a suitable site, hence the name of the festival. The storm clouds approached and a 5" deluge fell in not very long, and Joan Baez sang " We shall overcome " during a full on thunderstorm. Notable British performers there were Joe Cocker, which made his name, The Who, already famous. John Lennon was refused a visa- previous drug problems- and never appeared.Nor did Dylan, whose child was ill. Eight women suffered miscarriages whilst there.Nine out of 10 who attended smoked Marijuana and 33 were arrested on drugs charges. The organisers lost $US1.3m on the deal.

We all went Camping at the Woodstock copy cat Isle of Wight music festival that same year - with all the greats of the Era..Dylan, Stones, Hendrix, Baez, The Who- who that very year created the legendary "Tommy Walker " of Pinball Wizard fame- The Moody Blues. The list goes on. Fantastic!

However, 18 days later Hendrix was dead, drowned in a sea of his own vomit in Notting Hill, sick because of a cocktail of sleeping pills and red wine. Tragic!

By then I was living in South Kensington, working on my new career in Sales, playing serious rugby at Blackheath RFC and having a party time all the time I wasn"t working. Work was going well by now– I had a company Ford " Cortina " and the pay was brilliant. I was on my way.

CHAPTER SIX
FROM " COARSE " TO "FIRST CLASS" RUGBY

"They are the most useful players, the Dodgers ", who seize on the ball the moment it rolls out from the Chargers, and away with it across to the opposite goal; they seldom go into the Scrummage, but must have more coolness than the Chargers…"

TOM BROWNS SCHOOLDAYS

"Then there"s the fuddling about in the public house, and drinking bad spirits and punch, and such rot-gut stuff. That wont make drop-kicks or chargers of you, take my word for it…"

TOM BROWNS SCHOOLDAYS

"You"ve got to get your first tackle in early, even if its late"

RAY GRAVELLE, welsh rugby international

Rugby has been a passion of mine since I was 11, arrived at my new senior school, and couldn"t find any football (Soccer) pitches, a game at which I had been somewhat proficient at Junior school, and had been the Captain of the Team.

"No soccer here Sunshine." said the Grounds man, "Only Rugger"– Rugby Union.

I used to love soccer with a Passion and if I may say so I was good at it. This was the first I had heard about this and was not pleased. My

Dad hadn"t mentioned it. I felt I had been stitched up. Of course I hadn"t- my father had sent me to this excellent school with the best of intentions. Then a funny thing happened- within a year I was as passionate about Rugby as I had been about soccer. I also got into the "A"" Team in my year and if I may say, somewhat immodestly, I was good at it too. Took to it like a "Duck to water ", particularly for someone who hadn"t wanted to play it in the first place. For most of my school years I was the equivalent of a "Charger"- a flank forward, No.7. I got my Team colours in this position. Later on I became a "Dodger"- a "Back ". Because I was fast (fairly) and could score tries (statistically a matter of record).

Rugby is the " Beastly game   played by Gentlemen", whereas " Soccer is a Gentleman"s game played by beasts, a quote from someone called Henry Blaha, often misquoted. You must make your own mind up about this, but many people would agree that Rugby players" general conduct on and off the field is more gentlemanly, generally speaking, than soccer players", albeit they are no angels. But they take their knocks, don"t blame the referees for their misfortunes and don"t bear grudges. Rugby is the game where the players only stay down if they are REALLY injured, unlike "Fairy Footballers" who writhe around in apparent agony when there"s nothing wrong with them. Personally, I regard this as cheating, not that Rugby players don"t cheat from time to time. "Blood gate "– feigning a Blood injury to allow a proficient kicker back on the pitch at the Harlequin club is an ongoing controversy as I pen these words. Actually in my day the game was rather dirtier than it is now- much fairly gratuitous punching in particular- as there were rarely TV cameras about to catch offenders. Rugby players are also friends with the opposition and have a drink with them after the match– virtually no matter what has happened on the pitch. Footballers definitely don"t do that.

Surprising though it is to learn, upon research, one finds that whoever the game was invented by, it certainly was NOT Rugby School"s William Webb Ellis (WWE), he of the anecdotal and rather romantic story of when he allegedly " Picked up a football and ran with it, thereby "inventing" the game " . Even if "WWE" actually did this, he still didn"t invent the game as such. Research tells me various crude forms of rugby were springing up here and there around the world over some thousands of years from the Greeks, to the Welsh, and even the Cornish, where there exists a great rugby tradition to this day. It appears the Romans also played it here in the British Isles before they left our land to the Angles and Saxons. In some versions in the 1800s, the try was deemed invalid unless followed by a successful kick at goal, teams were at least 20 a side, and old versions of the game could last up to 5 days!! History tells us it is the case that Rugby School did produce an early version of the official Laws of the game, and is in other ways associated with its development, for example, change of ends at half time (to even things out when sunny or windy), and the type of ball to be used. Tellingly, "Rugby " Football carries the school name. Certainly, however, the pupils of Rugby school spread the developing game throughout England and the colonies when they left the school, so much is owed to them.

After school I turned out for the School Old Boys 1st XV. The Old Citizens– Old boys of the City of London School. I was 17 years old and they put me on the Wing which had become my main position. The club wasn"t very high ranking in the scheme of things– nevertheless a cut or two above "Coarse Rugby ". I loved the game and the people. And I came to love the club, which sadly no longer exists. Some years later, the   club lost their ground through mismanagement and the school,ironically from my viewpoint, reverted to soccer sometime in the 80s, so they lost their feeder anyway. The company was very good, some of my old school class mates playing in the team, and Saturday evening would usually, in those days, go on through. Saturday was rugby day. Girlfriends came second and could only come with us if they agreed to make the Teas. Clearly the average Rugby club was a bastion of male chauvinism in those days! We had an old fashioned skittle alley in our clubhouse which was fun, particularly when pissed, but the "Boot " was the best clubhouse game after matches.

A large glass "Boot ",which took about 3 1/2 pints of Bitter, was filled and several of us stood around in a circle. The game was to drink as much as you liked- a sip or a whole lot more - as it was passed around the group, but the PENULTIMATE person to empty the "Boot" had to pay for the next one to be filled up, and the whole process would start again. It was a game of inconsiderable skill and tactics but the idea was to leave as much unfinished as you could when it was your turn to ensure, if you could, that the bloke AFTER you was unlikely to finish it himself OR to finish it off yourself so the bloke BEFORE you lost the game.

One Saturday night, I stood next to this big fat "Prop Forward" who was, as it turned out, a big drinker. No matter how full the "Boot" still was, he managed to finish it off and I had to pay. He"d then go and be sick to make room for more and still do it again…. and again….I couldn"t believe it. 4 TIMES HE FINISHED IT OFF, TWICE FROM ONLY SIPS HAVING BEEN TAKEN BY PRECEDING DRINKERS including me. Extraordinary! Very expensive night for me that was as there were 9 of us around the "Boot" circle–that"s 31 and a half pints!

Another night I had a bet with Bills new girlfriend Sylvia that I could down a Pint quicker than her. Showing off I suppose. I couldn"t! She had that knack of opening her throat and pouring it in. I didn"t. Very embarrassing at the time, and caused much mirth amongst the Gang. Rugby players usually have clubhouses to drink in, unlike many amateur footballers. Unlike football, Rugby players at whatever level respect the referees, usually calling him "Sir". I did a bit of Reffing myself, after I finished playing at the notably late age of 50 years, and they even called me "Sir".

My first Captain was a previous Head Boy and Prefect at the school who had caned me for some misdemeanour or other years before. Yes, even Prefects caned errant boys at our school in those days, as at many other "Public "schools. His name was Geoff Coulson and his nickname was "Tromper"- I can"t remember why. Maybe he farted a lot. He was a Solicitor. We became great friends. He remains the most injury prone back row forward I ever played with! He was Captain that first year. My Dad became the "Bucket " Man- he came on when someone needed the ultimate cure for an injury, the magic cold sponge. He loved that club and they loved him. So much so that when I moved on some time later to a bigger club, he was not best pleased, and didn"t come with me for some time!! The "Old Boys " was "Coarse" rugby at its best but great fun and good learning. The" warm up "was a few fags, and the "warm down "was several pints and even more fags . The changing room was always full of smoke. Training was an hour in the school gym in the City once a week if you could be bothered to turn up (some couldn"t or would just come for the drinking afterwards) followed by, yes you"ve guessed it, a few pints and chain smoked fags. In truth we were never "Fit " as such. We didn"t know it at the time and we couldn"t have cared less - we were having a good time, were me, Chopper, Smithy, Ginger, Ships, Jonesy , Tromper et al. Great Easter tours to East Anglia, the south coast or the west country where we would play three matches , try and shag the waitresses in the hotel or the locals, drink gallons of Bitter or genuine "Scrumpy ", play silly drinking games and " Liar Dice " and sing classic Rugby songs like the "Engineers song":

"An Engineer told me before he died that he had a Wife with a C..t so wide that she was never satisfied.

So he built a Bloody great wheel, on it put a Prick of steel. Two Brass balls were filled with cream and the whole bloody issue was driven by steam, Ho Hum…Round and round went the bloody great wheel and in and out went the Prick of steel.", and so on…ending

" Now we come to the tragic bit, there was no way of stopping it ….she was split from arse to tit and the whole bloody issue was covered in shit!!!!

And "If I were the Marrying kind"..

"If I were the Marrying kind, which thank the Lord I"m not sir,the kind of man that I would wed would be a Rugby full Back

And he"d find touch and I"d find touch and we"d both find touch together

We"d be alright in the middle of the night finding touch together"

"If I were the marrying kind etc..
The kind of man that I would wed would be a wing three-quarter
"and he"d go hard and I"d go hard
We"d both go hard together"
And so on ……

and "Barnacle Bill the Sailor"..

WOMAN"S VOICE:
Who"s that knocking at my door?
Who"s that knocking at my door?
Who"s that knocking at my door?
Cried the fair young maiden.

MAN"S VOICE:
Oh, it"s only me from across the sea.
Cried Barnacle Bill the Sailor.
WOMAN"S VOICE:
Why are you knocking at my door?
Why are you knocking at my door?
Why are you knocking at my door?
Cried the fair young maiden.
MAN"S VOICE:
"Cos I"m young enough, and ready and tough.
Cried Barnacle Bill the Sailor.

Will you take me to the dance?
To hell with the dance down with your pants.

You can sleep upon the floor.
I"ll not sleep on the floor you dirty whore.

You can sleep upon the mat.
Oh, bugger the mat you can"t f*** that.

You can sleep upon the stairs.
Oh, f*** the stairs they haven"t got hairs.

What"s that running up my blouse?
It"s only me mitt to grab yer tit.

You can sleep between my tits.
Oh, bugger your tits they give me the shits.

You can sleep between my thighs.
Bugger your thighs they"re covered in flies.

What if we should get the (clap!)?
Gotta be willin" to take penicillin.

What if I should have a child?
We"ll drown the bugger and f*** for another.

Etc etc.You get the idea..

We could barely crawl onto the pitch the next day .

On my first Easter Tour, to Brighton as it happened, we stayed at the legendary Actress Dora Bryan"s hotel on the seafront. She of that great film "A Taste of Honey " and many a West end stage production. She and her husband and the Chihuahua were in the lounge to greet us as we arrived. They seemed pleased to see us.

"Where"s the Bar " someone asked, and we all piled in and got started. It was 3pm Easter Thursday.

Dora must have begun to fear the worst but she had no idea. At 11pm they rather optimistically closed the Bar and proclaimed that was it and no night service available. They wanted to go to bed and clearly thought we had had quite enough to drink by this time. We were, it has to be said, well pissed already, but they clearly had not had a touring rugby team there before and hadn"t a clue as to rugby player"s desire and capacity for drink and general rowdiness, and, therefore, what they had let themselves in for. Rugby boys on tour have certain expectations, and a night bar is definitely one of them. Actually, and quite sensibly, many hotels won"t take rugby tours—I"m not surprised! I wouldn"t either if I ran a hotel!

"What"s going on?" said our Skip?

"That"s it" says Dora, quite firmly.

"No that"s not it " says our Skip,"This is most unsatisfactory" somewhat more firmly, whilst we all stood at the Bar holding the shutters up thereby preventing their close. Dora is about 5 " tall and no match for a rugby pack! There followed a standoff for about ½ an hour whilst our older players negotiated a deal, and we duly got what we wanted. Dora and her husband had realised they were up against an irresistible force, and it was going to be much easier to give in. Drinking duly recommenced. To be fair, they would have made a small fortune behind the bar that weekend.This was something that surely dawned on them as the hours elapsed. Shortly the singing would start. Eskimo Nell, Craven A ("Never heard of fornication, playing with his Tool"), The Engineers song, and the rest of them. This would not be pleasing entertainment for the other guests. Sadly these days, to hear singing in a rugby club is more of a rarity, although it does still go on, in between the "Intellectual" conversations amongst the front row forwards. I think we went to bed in dribs and drabs from 2 am onwards- after all, we had a big match the next day- and to be fair "Hubby " stayed up to indulge us all that time! He had definitely got the message! He joined in with some gusto once Dora was in bed. It turned out he was pretty much "One of the boys " once she was out of the way, and , over time, had clearly been repressed by the formidable Ms B! Bill Lawton his name was, and he had been a well known professional cricketer in his day. This would explain it, as I know for a fact that cricketers in those days enjoyed their drink, Ian "Beefy " Botham being a notable, although perhaps extreme, example. Not like these days when "pro" cricketers have to take it rather steadier, obviously all except Freddie Flintoff that is. I"ve had a few with both of these icons myself, and was quite impressed with their capacity, although I"m not sure they know quite when to stop.

Anyway, Bill "s now sadly no longer with us, but we had a good laugh with him that weekend.Unsurprisingly, Dora never quite got used to us.

After the game the next day, and many pints later, well pissed, a group of us were staggering and weaving down the road in the middle of the night getting some fresh air after visiting a local nightclub, and took a fancy to some road-sign or other. Walking off with it along the Brighton seafront, it was intended to repatriate it to our clubhouse where it would receive a place of honour! I remember it was quite large and God knows how we were going to get it home, but no matter, we were having a right laugh! We hadn"t got very far when we were approached by a surly Policeman.

"What do you think you"re doing "? he enquired.

" We"re just re-locating this sign " we announced.

But we were going to be in trouble. Our big second row was a policeman and he was showing some concern to say the least. From the back one of our number, the inevitable "Tromper", announces:

"Its OK constable, I"ll deal with this. I"m a Solicitor "!

The Old Bill was so taken aback and unbalanced by this– that a Lawyer would be involved in such a childish, and certainly illegal prank- that in the end the only thing he could think of to say was:

" You better get on your way but put the sign back "

Which we duly did . What a hoot. God, how I miss those carefree days.

Soon after that Tour, the Rog and Howie got killed coming back from Spain–they also had played in the team- and for me the heart had gone out of the club and I needed a change.

BLACKHEATH RUGBY

"Lets fuck off to another Rugby Club" I said.
"Where to " ? asked Paul, our big second row and one of my best mates from School.
"Blackheath Rugby club "
"Don"t be a Cunt- we"re not that good at Rugby."
"No, but fuck it–lets go anyway " I said..

Actually, I didn"t think I had a prayer of making their 1ˢᵗ Team- maybe the 3rds if there were some injuries.
Anyway we needed a change so we made enquiries as to whether they would have us.

Blackheath was the biggest and best rugby club in Kent (still is) and one of the best in the Country. Dating from the 1850s, It is also the oldest open (ie without restricted membership) Rugby club in the world . Who did the first actual rugby club play against though? Rectory Field where the club moved to in 1883 (prior to which it played on the open Heath) is a truly historic place.It was developed thereafter by Blackheath Cricket club, (Rugby) Football Club and Lawn Tennis Company and became the home of Kent county cricket for some years as well. It is of historical importance as a sporting venue hosting many international rugby games; at one time, it was the unofficial home of the England national team along with Richmond Athletic Park before the development of Twickenham in 1910. The field is named after the Charlton Rectory that once stood at the site. The Club"s first opponents at Rectory field were Guys hospital. Leicester, HarleQuins, Wasps, Newport, Swansea, Saracens, London Scottish, Richmond, Gloucester and the great and virtually unbeatable London welsh were all on our fixture list, with at least 12 full internationals in the London welsh team including Dawes, Taylor, Mervyn Day, Gerald Davies, and the legend that is JPR Williams. British Lions to a man. Bristol, Moseley and many more famous names also adorned the List. Coarse rugby it was not. Nowadays Blackheath are in Division 1 (effectively National league 3) but In those days it was "First Class" Rugby.The best there was, albeit still an amateur game. Lets call it "Professional amateur". One of the clubs from which England"s Team were drawn. The Club had at least 4 internationals when I played there. It was legendary place and we realised a probably unattainable dream – I didn"t even know they would have us as members- perhaps drinking members which we knew we were good at having trained long and hard at it, but in truth I felt if they did we would be lucky to get into their 3rd Team and so did all our mates at the Old Boys Club. As it happens, one of our members at the Old Boys was distinguished ex -Blackheath player John Metcalfe and current Allickadoo member of the Old Boys. He and his wife used to lead the singing after the games at our club, an essential ingredient in coarse rugby. So I asked him what he thought.

"Great, fantastic, go for it, I will introduce you" was his astonishing reply.

"You probably won"t get in the first team " was his honest appraisal," but it"s a great place to be playing Rugby"

We joined the following summer and got straight to training with them. And we got stuck in. They ran 6 teams, so we were bound to get a game!

Proper training. For the first time in my life I got fit and faster. Though never the fastest as such I had some good moves! And I LOVED it there. Cutaway Adidas boots with aluminium studs for more speed were just coming out– at the Old Boys the studs were always leather and the boots covered the ankles. I immediately made an impact by crash tackling (Yes!) and hurting the pride of their star Fly-half, Les Byrne, an Under 18 England international tipped for a full England cap, in a pre–season practise game. Co-incidentally he had been a work mate of one of my mates killed in that car crash, and we talked about Roger and soon became friends. Roger had always been going on about him and it was now extraordinary that we were to be team mates. Rog would have been proud of me and not a little astonished that I was actually playing with Les!

Wonderful fraternity, the rugby world. You can literally turn up at any club in the world and be made to feel welcome.Instantly. And they did at Blackheath. "The CLUB " as it is known.

My first game was for the 5th team -predictable. On the wing. Not fast but tricky. Good hand-off and side-step–not my words.

But I progressed upwards over the next month and soon found myself in the seconds.Wow! The 2nd team! Exceeded expectations– mine and everyone else"s - by a street already.

My first game for the 2"s was at Oxford university 2nds (Greyhounds) away at the legendary Iffley rd ground, home also of the famous running track where Dr Roger Bannister had broken the 4 minute mile barrier 15 years before. We won the game and I scored a good, even great, try– miss one,   burst past their centres,   used our fullback as a dummy, round their fullback and in under the posts. Best try I ever scored for "The Club" they say. A few celebratory drinks at the famous University Students club "Vincents "...very POSH with leather chairs and ornate wooden pillars and wood panelled walls. Then into the car, and headed homewards to London. My car was now an Austin 1300. Stopped by the police.Whoops, speeding. Get a ticket. Probably lucky they didn"t spot the alcohol on my breath. It has to be said it was a bit more relaxed in those mid sixties days, although the new breathalyser system had just been announced by Barbara castle– October 1967- before which random tests such as standing on one leg or walking in a straight line were the normal tests . Still, I didn"t care too much– I was in the 2nd team, had played well and scored a great try.

Then, unbelievably, two weeks later,

" Peter Thorne"s out with knee ligament and cartiledge problems. We want you to play for the first team ".It was the skipper, David Webster, on the "Bone".

Thorne was a Legend. The previous season, Peter had a call from the England management to play against Scotland at Twickenham. A first Cap.

"Which wing am I on? " he had enquired.

"The left "

"Sorry, I"m a Right wing" he said.

So what? Its England on the phone dummy– play Prop if they ask you. I would have.

"Yes but Saturday you"re on the left. So and so, an established player, plays right wing "

"No sorry "

And that was that. He just couldn"t be persuaded and they chose someone else (Keith Savage, who went on to become a great player for England and a British Lion). A year later Thorne"s lying in hospital after a serious cartilage operation and I"m in the Blackheath 1ˢᵗ Team in his place.

"Are you taking the Piss "? I enquired of our Skipper.

"No "

"Sorry, you must have the wrong number," I said.

But remarkably he hadn"t. I was IN. I must admit to just a touch of "Schadenfreude" at that point for which I think I may be forgiven. Thorne never played again. That was sad .He was an excellent rugby player, even though he had been a Charlton Professional footballer before he found rugby rather late in life. On the other wing was my new South Kensington Flat Mate, Mike Bulpitt, who subsequently played for the Barbarians and once for England. I had moved out of home in Orpington into a new and exciting life at the centre of the action in London-into Mike"s South Kensington flat. My Mother said she couldn"t understand why I had stayed at home for so long, and seemed glad to see me go. ! was twenty years old and things were destined to hot up nicely over the next few years.

By this time, Paul had given up rugby for the time being to manage a pop group. We are, of course, still friends 40 years later and I was his best man for his 70s wedding to the lovely Rosemary . One of my only friends to stay married to the same person. Well done you two!

"Bustler Sumner faces Swansea" it said in the London Evening news.Whatever that means. Against Swansea , representing the might of Welsh rugby at that time. Match being played at home. We had three England internationals in our team(later five when Bulpitt and Tony Jordan were "capped") Simon Clarke, most capped England scrum half of the day until my old friend Steve Smith took the record off him many years later, Peter bell, back row, and prop Tony Horton who was also a British Lion. And I did face Swansea . And I scored a fucking try on my debut! How about that! And we drew the match. I got a punch for my trouble– fucking Welsh.But hey, I didn"t care.

The next season we were AWAY at Swansea. Got a thrashing as it happens. The Welsh are a different prospect altogether at their gaff. Welsh sides were renowned for the robustness of their forward play, especially at home.

The cry goes up: "Never mind the ball, get on with the game ". Horton, our British Lion prop, got his ample nose spread across his face with a furtive punch early in the game and never played rugby again. Tragic.

On the train to London Paddington coming back, our Skipper pulls a bird- quite fit as I recall- no more than half an hour out of London. We were all a bit pissed by then of course, to say the least. When we get off the train, he brags he"s just shagged her in the toilet.

"Bollocks " says the Hooker

"Lying cunt " adds one of the Props, rather unnecessarily.

Highly intellectual our front row was.

"No, straight up says the Skipper.

"Right, says the Hooker:

"Pull your knob out and if it smells of cunt, you have "

And he did. In the middle of the platform at Paddington station at midnight, the Hooker bends down and smells his prick _ it could ONLY be a front row forward who would do that. And it DID and he HAD shagged her! What a boy.

JAIL

Anyway, a month after my 2nd team debut at Oxford University, I was back at Iffley Road to play Oxfords Varsity match 1st Team, but this time with our first team on a coach. Thank goodness for that- at least I wasn"t going to get an endorsement on my driving license this time! Little did I know what was to come to pass that extraordinary day.

It was, as it happened, a freezing cold day. The heating on the coach had broken. We all took to the pitch frozen to the bone. Not good preparation. Not a good outcome either. We lost. Against a bunch of fucking kids. Shit. Fuck it!

Still, to be fair, the 60s were a bit of a heyday for Oxbridge rugby– both Oxford and Cambridge sported internationals of one nationality or another, and the next year (by and large) that same Oxford side beat the touring South Africans. Famous NZ All black international Chris Laidlaw was their captain, at the University on a Rhodes scholarship, so you get the general idea. Its all very different now for the universities in the professional era. They are not nearly so strong so the teams are much weaker and the Varsity match is much less of a draw than it was in my day.

Anyway, back on the coach, and still no heating. We stop at various pubs en route to drown our sorrows to the annoyance of the driver who wanted to get home. Right wanker he was. We got well "Tanked up" but were still very cold. Then one of the lads takes the law into his own hands with disastrous consequences. He lights a fire in the coach to warm himself up, using that days newspaper, just as we were hitting the A40 road to central London.

Oh shit. The driver seemed to take offence at this. Surprise, surprise! He Stops the coach, puts the fire out and, bemused, phones his boss from a roadside telephone booth for instructions. They were still talking on the phone as we sped off! One of the other lads– a senior pro - had jumped into the drivers seat and we were off!

His name didn"t come out in court - famous Kent farmer Peter Bell, the England International – but we wouldn"t snitch to the ultimate annoyance of the Rozzers, as they would have chucked the whole "Book" at him, although we would have got off. " All for one.....". Anyway, all was going well until we hit Parliament square, at which point we were literally surrounded by several Black Marias (what we used to call police cars as, rather unimaginatively, they were all Black in those days). We were taken to Cannon Row police station and ALL charged with "Driving and taking away a vehicle we know to have been stolen." They took our fingerprints and put us in the cells for the night and everything. We thought it was quite amusing - for a while. Then the worst bit. It subsequently transpired that " If you allow yourself to be "carried" in such a situation ", you can be charged too, even if you weren"t driving. That"s the Law. OH SHIT! And of course you"ve guessed what happened next. Have you? We all had our driving licenses endorsed, and large fines levied, and I had somehow managed to have mine endorsed for the second time whilst returning from playing

Rugger against Oxford university, within a month, this time in rather stranger and unlikely circumstances. It all made the National Press.

December 1967 was a very expensive month and 6 points on the license.

Nevertheless, in typical style, we celebrated Christmas with a big Blackheath Rugby Club dinner in one of its favourite restaurants– Quaglinos in London"s west end. The other was the famous "Rules" Restaurant in Covent Garden.

NAME IN THE PAPERS

"Victory has a hundred fathers, but defeat is an orphan"
Count Ciano

Most of our games would get reported in the sunday and monday national press, so one had ample time to reflect on performances good and bad. My worst performance ever, I seem to remember, was against Rosslyn park away– down from Putney on the south circular road. Oliver Reed the actor was a famous, mainly drinking, member by that time, although he had played the game as a young actor and, true to type, was always in the bar!

I had earlier already missed a tackle on my opposite number when suddenly their full back hoisted an "Up and under " in my direction. I steadied myself to catch it somewhere near our 25 yard (22 metre) line. What happened next was a bit of a blur, but I was enlightened the next morning when I read Michael Nimmo in the Sunday Telegraph. He wrote: (and I"m paraphrasing)

" The ball went in the air towards the Blackheath line. Sumner, attempting a " Mark " , seemed to forget the formality of catching the ball and failed to gather. The ball hit him on the chest, bounced forward and was collected by Andy Ripley (author"s note: famous England number 8 with whom I was acquainted) storming through and all over Sumner. Poor Sumner"s shout of "Mark" was still echoing eerily around the ground as the " Park " fullback stepped up to take the conversion following the ensuing Try!!"

A rather better day– probably my best game ever - was against London Scottish a few months later when I scored two tries, even though we eventually lost the match after two mistakes by our captain–England international Peter Bell features again– gifted them two.

Roy Standring in the Telegraph:

"..Two of Bell"s passes were intercepted on the Scottish 25 by Simmie, who burst clear for tries ...later in the game a refreshing understanding between Sumner and Fly Half Hennigan injected fresh purpose into Blackheath"s game ... ...Sumner"s excellent linking with the fly half from blindside wing produced two excellent tries for him and almost three...Sumner"s tries suggested Blackheath have something to look forward to next season"..

Co-incidentally, Bryan Kerr, a local friend of mine these days at my Tennis club , was playing for "Scottish " in that game, as we discovered by chance a few years ago!

In the bar at lunchtime afterwards was my Dad who had reluctantly decided to come and see what this Blackheath rugby was all about(Remember, bizarrely, he had stayed at the Old Boys when I left).

"What did you think of my tries Dad " I said.

"Don"t know, "he said "I"ve only just arrived ".

It had been a morning game due to the fact there was an international match in the afternoon and he hadn"t realised this!! He had managed to miss my best game ever!

BERLIN

A while after this event, we went to Berlin on a Rugby Easter Tour with a difference, when we got a real sense of the Cold War. West Berlin existed as a political enclave and the unofficial 11th state of West Germany between 1949 and 1990 when the Wall eventually came down and German reunification began. To get there you could go by road subject to border checks, but the best way was to fly straight in by air or go via the so called "Corridor" through Communist East Germany by train to the totally isolated and divided Berlin, an island state inland, located right in the middle of what had become Communist East Germany. Part of Berlin itself was controlled by the West"s occupying forces (USA, France, GB) and partly by USSR who, because of their determination to get to Berlin first enabled them to claim large parts of Germany to the east and west of Berlin itself, resulting in dividing the German state into two, creating East Germany in their image and controlling it and East Berlin. Richard Burton starred in "The Spy that came in from the cold " and Michael Caine in " The Ipcress File " and the other Harry Palmer stories, that beautifully captured the essence of it all. Desperate attempts to escape -often unsuccessful resulting in escapees being shot as often as not - to the west and spies and all that.

The East German guards that got on the train and checked our passports were truly scary. We were hosted by the British Army in West Berlin- stayed in an officers transit hostel for free! Somehow a few of us were allowed, courtesy of the Army, into the Checkpoint for a brief glimpse over the Wall of the grey bleakness that was East Berlin. Westerners were generally not allowed to cross into East Berlin. No wonder so many (East) Germans and others died trying to cross into the west illegally. Weirdly we played Rugby in the Berlin Olympic stadium where Adolf Hitler had spoken to the adoring hordes and the black athlete Jesse Owens famously won his four Golds in 1936, much to the chagrin of Herr Hitler. So much for his "Aryans as the Master race " idea. We could almost hear the echoes of his notorious speeches in that famous stadium and the roar of the enthusiastic crowds. It was virtually empty for us of course. Erie.

West Berlin was a really exciting city in those days. Instead of feeling sorry for themselves and isolated from the rest of West Germany, they were having a great time. The Beer Kellers were unforgettable, the nightclubs jumping and the girls seemingly endlessly available. Memorable.

CEYLON

Some years later we toured post colonial Ceylon (Sri Lanka) pre season where Mrs Bandaranaike had just become the worlds first female Premier. What a great 3 week trip that was! Kandy, Temple of the tooth, Tea plantation– did all that! We were to play Ceylon (twice) an Army team, a University team and a touring Welsh team, amongst others. 6 games in all over the 3 weeks. When we got to Ceylon, they gave us a big handful of Rupees for "Expenses only"- these were Amateur days remember - to spend, and billeted us with various Dignitaries and members of the various rugby clubs. I and two others got the Manager of the National and Grindleys Bank, Colombo. His house was in the near suburbs of the city. Typical colonial situation– he had a fifteen room "Grace and favour " house with at least 5 servants. A bank manager with 5 servants!! Waiters waiting on us on the patio of his mansion, filling and re-filling our beer glasses without us even noticing, as we chatted to our Host. And what wonderful and generous Hosts they turned out to be. When not training, or playing,we spent quite a lot of our leisure time in The Colombo club– one of the oldest Gentlemen"s clubs in Sri Lanka and located in the eponymous capital city, which had been established by colonial Brits in the 19ᵗʰ century in the English tradition, and membership thereafter limited to Brits and Europeans, until Ceylon"s independence in 1948.This was another example of a colonial world slow to disappear. Bars, snooker, swimming pool, tennis, croquet, fawning waiters, the lot! We were later honoured with a "welcome" reception at the British Consulate! We   trained most days we weren"t playing, and got after the beer every night with the consent and connivance of our team management who joined in the fun. "Freddie" Flintoff eat your heart out, you should have been a rugby player. Although, come to think of it, pro rugby teams aren"t allowed to drink that much these days! We always say better to have played in our era, rather than the new, professional one! We had Steak and eggs for breakfast every day. Golf at the Royal Colombo Golf club, a superb venue, where my bare footed local Tamil caddy was a source of good advice for the average golfer and could pick a ball up between his big toe and one next to it! You try it! The Hosts and their friends did, however, have the good sense to have all their women chaperoned. Even so, it was one of the best trips of my life although one day on a tea plantation is more than enough (we spent 2 and ran out of things to do and say). We won all our games by some margin, and, ironically, in spite of all the food and booze, I never played better – so much for nutrition, no drinking and all that.

I remember catching some bug or other just before we left and was basically physically sick all the way back 24 hours on the plane. I got no sympathy   or support from the stewardesses, who just seemed interested in chatting the other players up. Murray, our itinerant New

Zealand flanker, shagged one of them when we got back-lucky bastard, I thought at the time. She was gorgeous. Unsurprisingly, the girls were not interested in someone who was throwing up all the time! I spent the next 4 days in bed, and was out for the count for two of them attended by my flatmate Doctor! I was exhausted and didn"t fully recover for weeks which spoiled my fitness training for the new season.This started badly and got worse with a serious ligament injury suffered in the first match of the new season against Old Merchant Taylors. Out for three months and struggling to get fit for the County season. A bad end to a great year– I had been playing so well our President, the legendary Peter Piper, even thought I might get a sniff of England Honours (honestly!)

TWICKENHAM

My most memorable Rugby moment was when selected for Wasps "7 " for the Middlesex sevens finals at Twickenham in front of 50,000 people. I had left Blackheath earlier that same season having fallen out with our new captain, England international Tony Jordan– let"s just say we didn"t see eye to eye(he was a right WANKER actually)

It was a real wrench after 4 years at "The Club", but my new club had been very welcoming and were a good team as they are now, so I had settled in well.

I felt so proud as I walked up to the national stadium carrying my rugby kit-it didn"t seem real! Unfortunately, my careful fitness plans were ruined when, after going to bed nice and early, my girlfriend Jenny kept me awake all night shagging! How unprofessional of me! Consequently I was a bit wobbly on the day! We played the holders, the legendary London Welsh 7, in the first round (JPR Williams, John Dawes, John Taylor, Mervyn Davies, Gerald Davies , Billy Hullin et al) and we were 18 nil up with 5 Minutes to go! I was playing in the forwards–propping against the legend that was JPR Williams! ("Bumble " David Lloyd didn"t believe me when I told him this!)

The crowd were screaming for us. They LOVED seeing welsh teams being put to the sword! Twice I had backed up our winger hoping for a scoring pass, but each time he used me as a dummy to score himself. Bastard! Never mind though, we were winning at Twickenham and unexpectedly so. But the Welsh staged a comeback and somehow we managed to lose to a last gasp try by the man himself, JPR, who I, and one of my team-mates managed to miss in a crucial tackle(for which I could blame my girlfriend?). I cant tell you how pissed off we were, but that"s why they were legends-they never knew the meaning of defeat! All this was recorded by the BBC and I was on the Television that evening, but I missed it drowning my sorrows somewhere no doubt.

I also played County rugby for a while(Kent) and that, in those days, was a bigger honour than now. An England cap, however, was never on, but then I never expected it to be. I played with and against many international players and as a fellow winger, directly opposite the likes of International greats such as David Duckham, Keith Savage, Welsh legend Gerald Davies, England player John Coker and Irish legend Heinz Foods very own Tony O"Reilly making a late comeback. He turned up for the game in his Rolls Royce with a driver. As I mentioned, I played representative Rugby for Kent, and also Public School Wanderers, charity team The Bosuns and was selected for the Anti Assassins tour of Canada in 1974, but couldn"t go due to a dislocated elbow that I suffered in a badly executed tackle at the Leek Rugby Club sevens that has troubled me ever since! It"s not an injury that I would recommend! I had done well to get as far as I had in the game and, looking back, I am very proud of my achievements.

THE VETS

When I eventually reached 40 years of age after a few years of not playing, I decided I was missing the game so I joined the truly legendary team of any proper rugby club- yes,you"ve guessed–the Vets . Short for veterans, not animal doctors! This was at my northern club Wilmslow, Cheshire, whom I had joined 15 years before after being transferred north in my job. They had been high flying in the early 70"s, able to compete with, and beat, the likes of Sale and Harlequins, and socially , and success on the pitch wise, they were as good as any club of which I had been a member . Sunday telegraph Northern club champions in my second year. So they had some quality , but now ageing, players to draw from and several of these players went on to play with me in the

Vets Team now we had all got older! The "Vets" are Rugby players who have seen better days. They are supposed to be over 40 but one or two are over 60, which is taking it all a bit far. Some are under 40 which is a trifle unfair but hey ho! Vets do play Rugby but not as we know it, but they can still DRINK, and they do. Gallons of the stuff topped off with jugs of G+T. They are the best drinkers in the Club - by far- and they spend the most money because they have the most money. They are older and, on average, earn more than the younger players. They are also the best Tourists. For them, the social side of the game is the thing really. They have been fitter (Vets rarely train at all–indeed training is rather frowned upon) and faster.Vets are VERY SLOW INDEED, but don"t realise how slow they have become! In their minds, they still have IT! The old adage very much applies in their case:

"The older I get, the better I was"

To be fair, the one thing they do have is experience! My lot had loads of "experience"! I played centre or fly half in the Vets– even back row sometimes– as wingers rarely see the ball in vets rugby. In this form of the game, Wingers are often assumed to be no good, as the position is usually a repository for people who can"t catch, cripples, old men, fill-in players and other non entities. In spite of the limitations, we won most of our games and it was all great fun. I was captain for a while and even got ex rugby international legend Tony Neary - a friend and tennis partner, many players Rugby hero, now sadly a fallen hero - to play for us. My Team were impressed when he walked into the changing room for his first game:

"What"s HE doing here?" someone asked.

"Playing for us " I said.

They couldn"t believe it, but there he was. They were gob smacked. In his first game being unfit and out of practise, he only wanted to play one half, so sat on the bench for the first . Macclesfield Vets, on seeing him sitting there, exclaimed:

"Christ, if he"s only the fucking sub, who the fuck is playing back row!!"(the answer was me!)

A distinguishing feature of Vets rugby is that it is often played amidst a cacophony of sound. Frenzied shouts of advice to colleagues and referee alike, cries of encouragement from the captain and others usually many yards away from the actual action. Insults shouted to all and sundry and chatter about anything to take their mind off the game and the pain they were in. The object of the game is to WIN but to WIN with the least exertion, and get to the Bar as quickly as possible.

Vets are a nightmare to Referee. I know, I went straight from being a player to a referee, and my first match was "Reffing " the Vets! Vets very rarely get a proper "Ref" who knows what he"s doing, as they are off doing more serious matches, so they usually get a non - member of the Referees Society -i.e. unqualified such as myself- from the club on whose ground they happen to be playing! Equally he is very rarely fit and so can often lag behind play, even though the players are rarely fit either! There is also usually a lack of touch judges which just makes the whole thing so much more difficult and they always get the worst, i.e. muddiest pitches, usually miles from the clubhouse. To be honest it felt very strange and I wasn"t sure of all the Laws (I must confess I"m still not and never really found out all that goes on in the front row of the scrum and anyway there are far too many Laws!) so, unsolicited, they helped me out, giving me loads of unwanted advice.(they don"t know the Laws either!) At that point I was way outside my "Comfort Zone ". Referees are very rarely really in charge as such during Vets games, which are often run by a sort of committee made up of senior players from both sides. Out of this, a consensus seems to develop. One particularly useless referee I remember, exasperated with two bickering sides, said, and I quote:

"There is only one referee on this pitch "

To which one wag replied "Well for fucks sake give him the fucking whistle then ".

On another occasion the Ref having lost control of the match said:

"Look here, there are too many refs on this pitch"

To which the response of another quick witted player was

"Yes, and you"re by no means the fucking best".

In my first game as Referee, acting on instinct, I very nearly picked up the ball and ran with it! I got better.

At their age, Vets are much better talkers than they are players, and they DO TALK a lot to each other and to the ref. They talked to me a lot less later on when I started to award penalties for excessive talking and sent one or two of them off for Foul Play!

"You were a Wanker as a player and you"re a Wanker as a Ref" one of my old team mates said to me once during a particularly tense game when I had penalised him for punching an opponent. Charming! I sent him off too, even though he had a point! The same fellow is now dying of throat cancer. We"re dropping like flies. It"s so sad.

Anyway, the idea is to not get caught if you"re going to do that sort of thing. After the game, instead of tea in the dressing room like everyone else, they had bottles of whisky, gin or even champagne available. I kid you not!

SUMMING UP

One of my favourite (allegedly) true Rugby stories features legendary Irish and British Lion Lock Forward and Captain, Willie John McBride, a giant of a man in every way. The scene was breakfast in New Zealand on the first morning of a British Lions Tour down under.

The waitress appears.:

"Bacon and eggs for me " says big Willie.

"Sorry sir, we have no bacon " says the alarmed waitress.

" What?" booms Willie– "3 million sheep and no fucking bacon?"

That"s the lovely Irish for you, I guess!

One of my other (true) favourite rugby stories encapsulates the spirit and the bonhomie of the rugby world and its great game as told to me by my good friend Steve Smith, who I"ve played both with and against, who is an ex -record holding England scrum half of the 80s, and was intimately involved in this famous incident.

England were playing against Australia at Twickenham in 1982.

It was half time, and suddenly, unable to resist the urge for some reason to do something outrageous , out of the crowd comes this very large chested and rather attractive young woman, who proceeds to take her top and ample bra off and swing it round her head. Her Tits were just huge! She turned out to be one Erica Roe aged 24, who worked for an art dealer in Petersfield and had attended the match with a group of friends organised by her sister. Her action was apparently not premeditated. Bill Beaumont, the amply proportioned Captain of the day (he has a big arse!) was giving his half time team talk in the centre of the pitch. Bill, who I have had the pleasure of meeting and playing against in the distant past, and, anecdotally, not one of the more interesting talkers even at the best of times, is in full voice trying to rouse his team mates to greater deeds in the second half! Now noticing his team, one by one, were distracted, and with his back to the actual streak itself, he enquired of Steve what the problem was. Steve replied, and I quote,

" Bill, there"s a girl that"s just come out of the crowd, wearing your Bum on her chest ".

Erica went on to great things on the celebrity circuit, where rumours of her kindness and generous affection towards men have resonated ever since ! Initially, her girlfriend was going onto the pitch with Erica but chickened out, thereby missing out on all the many good things that were about to happen to her friend!

I eventually became Chairman then President of Wilmslow Rugby club, did my bit in a difficult period for the club putting it back on its feet and heading in the right direction, found my successor and then retired.

I LOVED Rugby . Nothing EVER replaced playing the Game I love, and I would go back and do it all again if I could.

Even though I played until I was 50, I"m still not sure if I fully played to my potential!

CHAPTER SEVEN
ASPECTS OF SEX

" I blame my Mother for my poor sex life.All she told me was "The man goes on top, and the Woman underneath. For years my husband and I slept on Bunk beds."

Joan Rivers

"My wife is a sex object. Every time I ask for Sex, she objects."

Les Dawson

"My love life is terrible. The last time I was in a woman was when I visited the statue of Liberty"

Woody Allen"

"It is the height of bad manners to sleep with a woman only once "

Marc Boxer

On the train home from school one day, a Smart-arse Friend revealed the secrets of Masturbation. There"s always someone who knows more than you, isn"t there! He revealed the secrets of the   "Joddrell"–also known as " The Sherman" and went on to explain how it worked.

"I can"t believe it" I said, when he told me about it.

It seemed like a wind-up. Was I 12 or 13 or so? So, somewhat tentatively it must be said, we all tried it there and then on the train (yes, disgusting I know)– we had the carriage to ourselves- and the existence of spermatozoa was confirmed. My mate Paul looked on at all this with some disdain- wanking was clearly not a new thing to him, but he preferred to do his in private, and who could blame him. Over the next few years, I would occasionally set the alarm early some mornings to get one in before school. They said it could make you go blind, but does it make you go mad? Doubt it. Is Masturbation "Punished by God eternally"? I"m sure a lot of people hope not. The best method I found was, armed with the indispensable copy of Playboy or Mayfair, I would do it left handed–you sit on your hand until it goes numb and it feels like someone else is doing it for you! A friend of mine– a bit of a specialist it has to be said- tells me he used to use his music stand to rest the mags on to free up both hands. Brilliant! I would never have thought of that! About that time , another friend told an unsuspecting mutual friend of ours, a bit of a "Thicko", that orgasm was achieved by rubbing ones ear.Poor chap tried for hours. We laughed for weeks about it.

When I was about 15 or so, I found an interesting book lying around the house. I can"t remember what it was called, but it was clearly all about the "Birds and the Bees ", of course procreation and sexual matters. I was just flicking through it when my mother came in the room and I tried, without success, to hide it quickly as it was about naughty things.

"Oh, that"s Ok, its for you " she said.

But I was 16 for Gods sake and went to a sophisticated school with worldly wise other boys, and I don"t wish to brag, but I was pretty much up to speed on the subject matters by then. I thought it highly amusing that they would think I wasn"t aware by that age!

Of course there wasn"t the sexual freedom and awareness amongst teenagers in those days that there is today. Women were yet to gain their later freedoms and status as the following demonstrates:

This is what purports to be an actual extract from a sex education textbook for girls printed in the 60s in the UK (unattributed) that is freely available on the Internet:

"When retiring to bed prepare yourself as promptly as possible. Whilst feminine hygiene is of the utmost importance, your tired husband doesn"t want to queue for the bathroom .But remember to look your best when going to bed.Try to find a look that is welcoming without being obvious. If you need to apply face cream or rollers, do so after he is asleep, as this can be shocking to a man last thing at night! When it comes to the possibility of intimate relations with your husband it is important to remember your marriage vows, and in particular your commitment to obey him. If he feels he needs to sleep immediately, then so be it. In all things be lead by your husbands wishes. Do not pressure him in any way to stimulate intimacy. Should your husband suggest congress, then agree humbly all the while being mindful that a mans satisfaction is more important than a woman"s. When he reaches his moment of fulfilment, a small moan from yourself is encouraging to him and quite sufficient to indicate any enjoyment that you may have had. Should your husband suggest any of the more unusual practices, be obedient and uncomplaining but register any reluctance by remaining silent. It is likely your husband will then fall asleep so adjust your clothing, freshen up and apply your night time face and hair care products. You may then set the alarm so that you can arise shortly before him in the morning. This will enable you to have his morning cup of tea ready for when he awakes".

I kid you not!

An early sexual experience was with my first real Love, Jackie W, who was always around and sort of available in the 60s when we lived in Orpington. She was my Dream girl and lived just down the road and around the corner. I was certainly in love with her to the point of obsession for quite a time during my mid teens, but for whatever reason, we never became steady girlfriend / boyfriend and whenever I thought this was going to happen, she would pitch up with another boy. I could never pin her down to be just with me.

Then suddenly I"m on top and, joy, at last we are making love.

"I"m coming, I"m Coming Jackie," I scream.

Then I wake up and I AM Coming ! Wet dreams aren"t ideal, but they are better than nothing!

And then, one happy day in 1962 when I was 15 or so, she gave me that long sought after "Barclays Bank " in the woods near our home. I had watched her for years out of my Bedroom window walking home past our house.

"Poetry in Motion" she was. Sexy as hell in her choir girls robes and, as it turned out, very aware sexually speaking. But she had always seemed so unattainable- actually she wasn"t at all unattainable. I was so jealous whenever I ever saw her with another boy. On this particular occasion, we lay down beside a pre- harvest cornfield near our homes on a beautiful summer evening. At the same time, an older couple were just taking a stroll, and came upon this amorous scene where my trousers must have been down somewhere near my knees, my big arse showing, and her skirt some where up around her neck... whoops! We were both in the Church Choir, the Church Youth Club and the Athletics Club together. I was MAD about her and now I had turned my dreams into reality. My sex life had begun , although we didn"t actually have full sex that day and not for some time.

In the end, she became my first love subsequently scorned which I"m sure lead to a subconscious determination not to make myself so vulnerable ever again. Unfortunately, to experience true love and in my opinion, you have to!

Sexually speaking, and looking back, the biggest problem as a rampant teenager was that I went to a boys only school. The result is that for many years after I didn"t really know HOW to converse with women. I had actually got to know very few in my life. We all saw girls as sex objects- nothing more, nothing less, certainly not friends and didn"t really understand them at all as such. But we fancied (some of) them and put them on pedestals. I used to chat them up and in a rather clumsy way too, rather than just chat TO them. Women aren"t totally stupid- no, I"m not just saying it- and they picked up on this. My Children both went to mixed sex schools and University, so they know how to make friends with the opposite sex and converse with them even if they don"t want to "Shag " them! I never bothered with a woman unless I wanted to shag her. I"m a lot better nowadays, presumably maturing with age, and nowadays count quite a number of women amongst my friends.

After School, I went straight out to work and this had various side benefits:

A. One gets paid– no more paper rounds or gardening for Dad or

Neighbours which were much too much like hard work for little reward.

B. There are WOMEN there!

C. I didn"t have to go to school anymore- no more homework.

D. The downside is far less holidays

But how to go about pulling the women at work when one is obviously so crap at chatting them up?? And, I will confess, a little shy in those days. I had a lot to learn. One of the things I"ve learnt over the years is that its sometimes better to let them chat you up. That way, you don"t experience rejection! It is, however, a very limiting strategy because that"s not many (most?) women" s style. Look, just talk to them and see what happens! I was, when younger,a bit tongue tied where women were concerned and curiously lacking self confidence. I have learnt well! Early on, I mistakenly kept tapping the ugly ones for sex on the basis they would be grateful. Wrong.Oddly, subsequent research indicates its usually the "Lookers " that are the " Go-ers", as I eventually found out when I plucked up the courage with Jackie W . Funny and ironic that. Jackie W was around but I was always on the lookout for fresh talent and I was still effectively a virgin at 17, having so far failed to make love to Jackie, albeit the petting was going well. Pauline, who I met at work and lived in a semi in Grove Park– her father was a London Bus driver and as it happens pissed off that many of the incoming blacks from the Caribbean were themselves becoming bus drivers, which he felt demeaned his profession- was a lovely girl and quite attractive, but weeks of trying to " Get a bit off her" on regular dates with her led nowhere. Not even a "Bit of tit", let alone a " Sherman " or perhaps even more. This is how we used to think. I"m not proud of it, just being honest! Anyway, I was really trying, but she was certainly no Jackie W who could always be relied upon for a good bit of something or other. But I wasn"t getting anywhere with Pauline. Not so much as a "One off the wrist " after months of frustration. Very unsatisfactory. So, in the end, Pauline had to go. How shallow of me.

Through work, soon after I started my first job, I was invited to a party in Essex with some older girls in the office.

Armed with low expectations given their age, during the evening,I was amazed to be dragged to a bedroom by one of them, (clearly under the influence of cheap wine) who, much to my genuine surprise and not a little delight, proceeded to "Toss me off" with some enthusiasm. However, she nearly succeeded in ripping my knob off! Clearly an inexperienced hand!

"Slower and more gentle" I said, and she did oblige, but lets just say it was alright but she wasn"t very good at it. Mind you we men can"t talk- what do we know about the women"s best bits, where they are located, and what to do when we get there?

The clitoris–handle it well and you are IN! That"s if you can find it. Good luck with that. I"m reliably informed men–particularly young men - often make little attempt to find it, or look in the wrong place,and if they do find it, they rub it too hard and insensitively, not properly lubricating as they go. In my day most young men didn"t even know it existed, let alone find it, and I would have been the same. And your homework is to find the so called "G spot"- after the German gynaecologist Ernst Grafenberg …..if you can find it, you"ll apparently have her "coming " all night! Yeh right! (Look between 1-3 " up the front of the vaginal wall and it forms part of the female prostate so research tells me . I didn"t know they had one! Take a ruler and a telescope. I remember a rather pretty woman years ago who showed me where she thought hers was and indeed you might have fun looking for it..

There were some disappointments on the way, and some very good tries but, eventually, I managed to persuade someone - luckily a female - to have Sex with me . I was 17. She was 17. It was Jackie W of course.

I called her "Ever Ready " after the Batteries of the same name, as she was always available for a fumble. I adored her and had looked upon her as "Forbidden fruit ". She was beautiful- slim, long, dark, almost black hair, not tall-probably 5" 3" from memory- and perfectly in proportion. We went up to her bedroom when her Mum was out at work. We undressed and lay close side by side. We kissed passionately. I ran my hands over her smooth back and squeezed her small breasts and tight bum. I ran her nipples through my fingers and licked them. I seemed to be doing the right things– I had seen the odd Bridget Bardot film - but I was not relaxed and I was experiencing a degree of "Performance anxiety". I was, however, now "Living the Dream and I needed to get it done. I pinched myself to ensure it was now the real thing. She was breathing heavily. I was in Heaven. I touched her vagina and ran my fingers inside as I had done many times before.. She was very wet. She stroked me gently, just how I like it. I was getting very excited and I feel it"s the right time– how does one know - so I fumbled for a condom. Then, disaster . I got so excited, I "Came "while I was putting the condom on! We all know about "Premature ejaculation", but this was ridiculous! Not an impressive debut!

"How was it for you?" I said, trying to make light of it !

To say she was disappointed after ages, as it turned out, waiting for me to make the move, is an understatement. Embarrassing! Nevertheless, it was start, albeit a faltering one, and she did give me another chance once I had rested for a bit. After all, step forward the man who gets it right first time–or even second time??

These are faltering steps for many men– a well trodden path of failure followed by triumphant success!

Of course , one doesn"t hear parallel stories of failure from ones mates–their failures are kept well under wraps:

"I fucking gave "er one, no problem. Shagged all night ".

So you are bound to think only you are having these problems. Not a bit of it!

The next time was more satisfactory- not brilliant mind- and it all got better with practise of course although there are practical aspects concerning the use of condoms. For example, when does one ideally put it on? How does one keep her excited whilst putting it on? It can"t be done one handed that"s for sure! Of course they are appropriate protection in many scenarios, but I cant say I"m much of a fan of condoms myself!

Just en passant as it were, whilst we are on the subject , you might be interested in the origins of the condom itself? In fact, the history of condoms is one dating back thousands of years to the ancient Egyptians.

A drawing of a sheath being worn like a condom was discovered that dates back 3,000 years to the Egyptians of 1000 BC. These sheaths were worn to protect from disease. Europe was first introduced to condoms a thousand years later around 100 AD as seen in paintings within the caves of Combarelles in France. Some evidence exists of condoms being used in Imperial Rome. It was the widespread European syphilis epidemic in the 1500s that gave us the first written condom reference, attributed to the Italian Gabrielle Fallopius. In his writings, Fallopius claimed to be the inventor of these early linen sheaths that would be safeguards against the deadly syphilis virus. These early condoms were used only to protect against disease and nobody had yet worked out their incidental, but no less important use, as protection against unwanted babies. It is thought that Casanova was a regular user of condoms.

Then importantly, in 1844, Charles Goodyear (of Goodyear rubber tires) perfected and patented the process of vulcanizing rubber. This process transformed normal rubber into a material that was both flexible and strong. In turn, condoms were able to be mass-produced, making them more affordable and more available to the masses. Latex condoms emerged in 1919 bringing with them the advantage of lasting longer, smelling less offensive and being thinner.

Jackie and I never became steady Girlfriend/ Boyfriend as such, and a while after our first few shags , she started going out with a boy rather older than us -25 I think- who had things to offer I couldn"t match.Like money and a car. I was not yet the proud owner of a motor, and my earnings were very small compared to his. When she was 18, about a year later, Jackie married this fellow, a Mining Engineer, and went to live in Zambia for a few years. Deep down I was heartbroken.

When she came back a few years later, I bumped into her quite by chance. She had divorced, surprise, surprise, and seemed available. By then, I was living in South Kensington with some of my Blackheath Rugby team mates . It was 1970. We went to the cinema to see the film of one of my all time favourite books, "Catch 22", in which the World War 2 US Airmen, whose colleagues were dying by the day doing mission after mission, couldn"t apply for repatriation to the USA unless they were "Mad " and, if you had the presence of mind to ask, you clearly weren"t "Mad " in the first place. This was the so-called "Catch 22". Two of my favourite characters in that book were "Major Major " (played by comedian Bob Newhart of "Driving Instructor "fame) with whom, somewhat perversely, you couldn"t have a meeting until he was out of his office, when of course he wasn"t available anyway. Then the wonderful rant against capitalism provided by Milo Minderbender, played by the ever excellent Jon Voight, and his dodgy commercial deals with the enemy - such as allowing the airfield to be bombed by the German Air force, Approved by the complicit General Dreedle, memorably played by Orson Welles. Nately"s bizarre love relationship with a local Italian Hooker is also worthy of note. Brilliant!

Anyway, Jackie and I got on really well and spent the night together. It was bliss and all the memories came flooding back, but I had moved on. I never saw her again.

My Sister was a good source of crumpet for me. She went to a Convent school in Southeast London and, trust me on this, these are the best sex academies out there! They seem to be hotbeds of repressed sexuality and there existed amongst the girls a rebelliousness,probably caused by all that contact with Nuns, that can be turned quickly to one"s advantage . I got a regular supply of girls from my Sis over the years, including the lovely "D", who was excellent at BJs, but didn"t want to do much else. Ok by me. Sis herself in her early days as a student Physiotherapist, would earn spending money providing "happy Endings " in a massage parlour in Chelsea. Ok, I don"t know this for a fact (actually she denies this) but you would wouldn"t you?

One night stands? I"ve had a few. Quickest I got a woman to bed was an hour after meeting her. Did she get me into bed or was it vice versa? Was she a Slag? Was I a Slag? Both of us? Society seems to have it the Man"s a Stud and the Woman the Slag in such an encounter. That does seem very unfair to me. I feel I"m definitely a "Slag" as well. Of course , women can be just as predatory as men, in my experience, and, confronted with a clear proposition from an attractive woman(if I happen to notice the signals that is) I am completely defenceless. I am like putty in their hands. Seems rude not to really! So be vigilant -there are plenty of "Cougars" about who would have you stray from the straight and narrow.

I don"t feel it"s an idle boast to declare that I regard myself as having been moderately successful with women over the years but, to be honest, I"ve never really been sure about casual sex. It can be a bit of a minefield if you ask me. With a stranger there were, and always are, things that might blow up in your face.

Firstly, the physical matters. A period of anxiety before the first sex with a new woman. Will she be offended if I try it on? Or offended if I don"t? Was one too small, or too big (fat chance), too limp, too quick to come, too slow to come, or not come at all! What does she like? Should I ask her? Should I suggest a condom? At what point in proceedings does one put the condom on? Does one arrive wearing it? One of my mates did just that to a party we all went to when we were 16 and he assured us he had been promised a shag by this particular girl. As it turned out, she chickened out or maybe he did. Too many things to go wrong, and by the time I was 21, I had experienced most of these " Procedure failures ". The worst is not getting a "Hard on ". Erectile Dysfunction" (ED) also known as "Impotence ". This is, of course, often caused by anxiety and exacerbated by alcohol. Or you may be genuinely unable to ever get a hard–on, in which case my sympathies–it must be shit. ED is bad, partly because the exercise cannot proceed, and partly because the woman takes it as a personal slight, and you may not see her for dust after that. Premature ejaculation(PE) comes a close second. PE has, for me, very occasionally been a problem over the years, in particular with any new sexual partner when I usually get over-excited which is hardly surprising, let"s face it! In fact it is one of the commonest sexual problems, suffered by many men from time to time. At least 30-50% of men have suffered! No, it is NOT a condition suffered by women, so they really don"t understand the problem. It may be caused by over excitement, over sensitive sex glands or, according to psychologists, subconscious feelings of guilt or concerns about being caught when masturbating as a youngster. Ah yes, that will be it! I think all of those may apply to me, as it happens. In any event, it often appears to be rooted in psychological issues. When "PE" occurs of course the woman is not going to enjoy the experience as by the time you have climaxed she is, in effect, only just getting started. Again, as with "ED", she is not going to be best pleased. I"ve had one or two unfortunate experiences in this area in my time I"m embarrassed to say. Most men have. That said, she should be flattered that she got you so excited you came so quickly! (She usually ISN"T flattered– just disappointed or annoyed !) A cure for this unfortunate condition? No idea– maybe get started and then imagine you are with your wife(only joking) or the ugliest bird you ever met? There are organisations out there who claim to be able to cure it, but I haven"t got around to finding out. Of course, It"s a bit late now to bother!

All that said, my own sexual preferences are relatively conservative with a small "c". More Missionary than Canine.

More "Flamingo Road" than "Cadbury Way" so to speak. When it all comes together (Sic) the pleasure is all too fleeting, albeit it undoubtedly gets better with practise. Rather sadly for most of us, within a marriage sex becomes rather routine and thus the magic does tend to fade over time. I"m sure its partly this that leads to so many divorce cases.

The sex life and sexual habits of the inhabitants of these islands has taken different forms over the centuries.

Were you aware, for example , of the following :

Kissing as we now know it wasn"t practised until 15th century although the practise, predictably, did not fair well for a while under the Puritans two hundred or so years later. With the Restoration (of the monarchy) in 1660 it made a bit of a comeback under King Charles 11. In the period leading up to the 19th century the English were regarded as the most beautiful of peoples due to their lack of tendency to inbreed in the way our continental cousins did and our keenness on outdoor sport and other pursuits keeping us healthy. 19th century women were very forward. Until the 19th century, courting couples in Wales were allowed trial nights of sleeping together!

Up to the end of the 19th century there was a practise called "Bundling" which involved young lovers "Courting horizontally " in bed as it was often too cold to do it anywhere else. With the full knowledge of the parents, they would go to bed together with their clothes on and it was supposed to be above board–yeh right! Practising "Bundling " with Frances Dereham, Thomas Culpepper and others in her youth before and after meeting and marrying King Henry V111 cost the highly sexually active and experienced fifth wife Catherine Howard her head, and that of the unfortunate Culpepper, when the King eventually found out. Dereham was hung, drawn and quartered for defiling Henry"s Queen all those years before he met her himself.

Lonely Hearts ads in newspapers are not new– the first appeared in 1695!! In the 18th and 19th century, high class married women would seek out discreet places of ill repute to indulge their sexual fantasies. I guess they still do?

It seems we didn"t invent sexual freedom in the 60s and this is confirmed in the next section of my book!

In 1948 the famous "Kinsey report " was published followed by an even more controversial sequel in 1953.

Kinsey, a teacher of Biology at Indiana University, realised his students knew very little about sex and actually many feared it. 40% of them thought masturbation caused insanity!

So he resolved to research these matters and the reports were subsequently published.

The main findings were:

85% of white males had had premarital sex.

50% (yes 50) had had extra-marital sex

And 69% (yes!) had visited prostitutes.

63% of women masturbated and 14% were capable of multiple orgasms. Half of women had had premarital sex and of those, 77% had no regrets.

A nymphomaniac, he contended, was someone who has had more sex than you!

And all this in 1948 America!

Much later in the last century, various studies on penis size were done. One such, conducted amongst 50 women, concluded as follows:

"When people speak of penis size, they typically refer to length. Thus, a man with a short but wide penis would probably think of himself as having a small penis, and would be so thought of by others, too. However, width is part of size, although usually not acknowledged. Does width contribute to female sexual satisfaction? 45 out of the 50 female students surveyed spoke of width being more important than length."

" It is not obvious why a wide penis would be preferred to a long penis, but speculation would suggest the following. Penis width may be important due to a penis thick at the base providing greater clitoral stimulation as the male thrusts into the female during sexual intercourse."

But perhaps size is unrelated to female sexual enjoyment?

The famous 1950s and 60s sex researchers Masters and Johnson concluded "that size of the male penis can have no true physiological effect on female sexual satisfaction."

They base this conclusion on their physiological studies that show that the vagina adapts to fit the size of the penis. Because of this vaginal adaptation, they refer to the vagina as a potential space rather than an actual space. Thus, despite the worries of many males about the size of their penis- no comment - Masters and Johnson concluded that any size penis will fit and provide adequate sexual stimulation to the female. The present study was conducted to see if female college students would report their sexual satisfaction related to penis length, width, or neither.

One thing I"m sure of is that many women would deride a very small knob, so I can only conclude that mine, whilst not large, is just about OK, as must be my technique I suppose!!

Masters and Johnson were the first to conduct research on the sexual responsiveness of older adults, finding that given a state of reasonably good health and the availability of an interested and interesting partner, there was no absolute age at which sexual abilities disappeared. While they noted that there were specific changes to the patterns of male and female sexual responses with ageing– for example, it takes older men longer to become aroused and they typically require more direct genital stimulation, and the speed and amount of vaginal lubrication tends to diminish with age as well– they noted that many older men and women are perfectly capable of excitement and orgasm well into their seventies and beyond. Well, that is good news …..!!

AFFAIRS

I"ve had a few……..BUT

Why do people have them even though many of these same people love their partner.? Having Mistresses was and is commonplace and (almost) respectable amongst the Aristocracy and upper classes. But WHY? Perhaps because, as I say above, sex inside marriage becomes routine and they miss the excitement of the chase. Quite simply, monogamous sex becomes less interesting over time and individuals of both sexes feel the need to prove they can still do it I guess. There are,of course, exceptions. Affairs are a taboo subject and the source of much hypocrisy. In the sex game who is using who? Whether its the bored businessman (or golfer!) looking for some excitement or the bored housewife with a boring husband looking for something- anything -putting temptation in the way of married men. Famously Hugh Grant, much in love with Elizabeth Hurley at the time and, as I write this, a happily married Tiger Woods has now been caught with his trousers down- almost permanently down by the sound of it,and the wails of hypocrisy can be heard across the world. John Terry Footballer. Ashley Cole footballer. Andrew Marr, respected broadcaster. All unable to keep their zips done up. Then there"s Leanne and Nick, Kevin and Molly and Peter and Carla, albeit in the fiction that is "Corrie ", but then "Art mirrors life " doesn"t it? Looking back into history they all seem to have been at it–adultery wasn"t invented in the 70s. Julia, daughter of Augustus Caesar, took many lovers. As did the wife of The Emperor Claudius, although in her case the drawback was he had both her and her last lover killed once the affair became the talk of Rome. You have been warned! Some figures I saw recently suggested some 70% of Men and almost as many women cheat on their partners. That"s a lot! I confess I can be included in this depressing statisitic.

One of the most famous affairs of all time was that between Lord Horatio Nelson and Emma Hamilton. Emma, Lady Hamilton (26 April 1765 to 15 January 1815) was born Amy Lyon in Cheshire, England, the low born daughter of a blacksmith, Henry Lyon, who died when she was two months old. She was brought up by her mother, formerly Mary Kidd, with no formal education. She later changed her name to Emma Hart. She lost her virginity at a relatively young age when one of her male relatives was co-erced. Later she sometimes worked as a nude model for Gainsbrough and Reynolds and may have even been a prostitute as well. When they eventually met after the Battle of the Nile, Nelson was already hugely famous, and had already lost his arm and most of his teeth. Emma had by then married the much older Sir William Hamilton, apparently as a marriage of convenience, and was living in Naples. Emma reportedly flung herself upon Nelson in admiration, calling out, "Oh God, is it possible?", as she fainted against him. Nelson wrote effusively of Emma to his increasingly estranged wife, Lady Fanny Nelson. Emma and Sir William, her husband, escorted Nelson to their home. Emma nursed Nelson under her husband"s roof, and arranged a party with 1,800 guests to celebrate his 40th birthday. They soon fell in love and their affair seems to have been tolerated, and perhaps even encouraged, by the elderly and now cuckolded Sir William, who showed nothing but admiration and respect for Nelson, and vice-versa. Emma Hamilton and Horatio Nelson were by now the two single most famous Britons in the world. They were not only in love with each other, but admired each other to the point of adulation. Emma, her husband and Nelson eventually lived as a "Menage a trois " in London , much to the consternation of the Court, from which they were then ostracized.

In the 19th century "most" married society men had mistresses, many of whom saw no need to keep the fact secret from their wives! A Century later, with convention demanding we keep these matters under wraps, we find even nice but "grey "John Major at it– who would have thought it and with whatser name Edwina curry– not my type. Michael Foot with someone as well! He never looked up to the job! Prince Edward (future Edward V11) had many mistresses and these were tolerated by his wife. Times have of course, changed, and seemingly there was always a different set of rules for Kings anyway!

Fact is many, probably most, men have at least one affair in their married lifetime–I have to admit that I have strayed several times - and many more have multiple affairs. Trick is not getting caught I guess. Nor confessing– why load her up with your guilt? Or him. I myself have known many married men and some married women who are constantly on the lookout. We don"t seem to be programmed for monogamy do we? The French seem to know this and the wives are said to tolerate it all, again, if discretion is applied. Sometimes it occurs that the man will dump his Wife and marry his Mistress. In the words of late billionaire industrialist Jimmy Goldsmith, a well known "Francophile" :

This "Creates a vacancy" (for a new mistress). Some people are just incorrigible.

It seems affairs can often be a bit of a "Safety valve " for a marriage. Certainly the French believe Affairs tend to keep marriages together rather than drive them apart.

The question arises " In truth, should monogamy be given such a supreme value? "

In the end, I suppose its up to the individual to decide what his or her values are to be but WHY do we spend so much time and effort into suppressing one of our most basic needs? It"s because its conventional to do so but possibly not natural? You decide!!

My advice is–try to be faithful, but if you cannot, keep it secret, don"t get caught, never confess, and get over it if you find out your own partner is at it, be you man or woman.

I,of course, did get caught!

PAYING FOR IT

This is nothing new–they say it"s the "Oldest profession ". Its not actually, as midwifery probably is, and lets face it, all men pay for sex in some way shape or form. God, how cynical I can be! In certain quarters, it was even considered respectable.

The first recorded Bordellos were in the temple of Babylon where women had sex for ritual not gain, whilst in Greece in 5th century BC they were run by the state and the women were taxed. The Romans were very keen on sex as we know. Waitresses in taverns often sold sex and official prostitutes were registered and regulated by the police. Rent from a Brothel was legal income. Later in history , the "red lights " tradition seems to have come from the days railwaymen left their lanterns outside whilst they were inside a brothel. Prostitution was tolerated in the middle ages as it was felt it was less of a problem than rape and sodomy. In 1161, Henry 11 allowed the regulation of Londons Bankside Stewhouses (Brothels). In France and Italy, and England Courtesans– an elite form of prostitution–flourished amongst the upper classes and were often admired. In 1546 Henry V111 tried to close the"Bawdy houses ", of which there were many, without much success. Originally legal in the USA, prostitution was eventually outlawed around 1915 in most states on the initiative of Christian women– but some counties in Nevada still have it as legal to this day. In the UK, prostitution itself is legal (i.e. paying for sexual services except by force and child prostitution and pimping) whereas keeping a Brothel is not. Clearly blind eyes are being turned towards most massage parlours!

Charles 2nds mistress Nell Gwynne began her working life as a Prostitute in a Mrs Ross" Bawdy House in Drury lane.

In Georgian London (18th century) it is estimated that 1 in 10 women were Prostitutes–about 50,000 - as there were few other employment opportunities for uneducated women at that time! Many plied their trade around the theatre district of Covent garden, their clients wealthy theatre patrons amongst others. Prices varied from £50

For a "Courtesan ", worth some £6000 in today"s money, down to a few pence - £2 today.

European Prostitutes flocked to London to work much as they do today but it was not always necessary to pick up street girls. A selection of women of a higher class appeared in "Harris"s list of Covent garden ladies ", a publication which appeared annually from 1760-1793. About 80 women appeared in each edition giving such detail as their address, age, accomplishments, physical attributes and charges. The cost of a full night with one of the ladies was about £2 in old money- about two weeks wages for the average ordinary working man. Ordinary working girls often prostituted themselves for money to supplement their pay. For example, Milliners, and Bonnet makers. The spread of the "great pox " or the "Spanish Pox " later called the "French Pox"–all terms for syphilis - throughout Europe at this time inhibited the spread of Prostitution and was caught by a surprising number of people, and, perversely and typically, for the French, it was regarded as a bit of a "Badge of Honour " .Syphilis allegedly arrived in England circa 1496 brought here by English soldiers fighting in Europe but there is some disagreement amongst Historians about this. Because of the people traffic coming through London, the disease took a real hold all over Europe, causing havoc as men gave it to their wives, and Mistresses and women to their husbands. The better Brothels had their girls inspected and certificates were provided to those free of the disease. James Talbot carried out a survey of Prostitutes in 1838. Of these, 3 were under 15, 414 between 14 and 20, and 29 between 50 and 60. At that time there were some 400,000 directly or indirectly involved in the sex industry in London, four times more than is estimated nowadays for the whole of the UK! In Victorian times, according to Talbot, there were some 5,000 Brothels offering many services including Child Prostitution which was very popular at the time. Girls were traded and trafficked all over Europe for the Brothels, so that"s nothing new. King Edward V11 himself was a known frequenter of Brothels along with many other members of the

Upper classes and Aristocracy. Prime minister Gladstone is said to have used Prostitutes his whole life, even when he was 70, under the guise of "saving fallen women". Wit Disraeli is said to have quipped:

"When you are out saving fallen women, save one for me ".

Van Gogh was heavily into Prostitutes and even had a baby with one.

It was regarded as just a bit of fun. Not socially unacceptable as it became in the UK over time, although this appears to be changing back. As I write, the Prime minister of Italy - Berlusconi - is reliably reported as having been at it with Prostitutes over many years.

There is now what I shall call the apparently socially acceptable new sport of "recreational " paid for sex. For example, 100s of stag weekends to places like Prague and Tallin, where literally thousands of handsome East European girls ply their trade(at least those ones who aren"t over here do!) in lap dancing bars and brothels. All this seems to be regarded by the, often but not always unmarried,younger generation as all harmless fun, but us Baby Boomers hardly ever did it in our day, presumably because it was not freely available as it is now and we were perhaps getting enough "free". It seems we are one of the only members of the animal kingdom who enjoy "recreational sex".The only others, so far as we know, are Bonobos, Chimpanzees and Dolphins! Anyway, be that as it may, we never dreamed of PAYING for it in those days but clearly men today, including celebrities and others think nothing of doing just that—it seems to have become some sort of accepted norm! There are some lovely girls plying their trade in the upper echelons of the sex industry, mainly in the better massage parlours -come on, who hasn"t had a "happy ending " massage? - lap dancing bars and in the "Escort" industry . In my experience, remarkably lovely some of them. Not sad or druggies but smart, attractive and know exactly what they are doing and even seem to enjoy it. They are doing it for a variety of reasons- enjoy sex and easy money, or have a kid and no partner and don"t want to sponge off the taxpayer(highly laudable!) and a myriad of other reasons. ExploitERS if you like NOT exploitEES! I do not include street girls in this who are to be avoided and are often druggies and sad generally. These are the girls always depicted on TV programmes, thus giving a false impression of the sex industry, insofar as I"m qualified to comment. High class Hookers ("Escorts" or "Courtesans ") are now "Coming out ". See Belle de Jour "s Book on her sex career now serialised on TV with Billie piper in the lead role– Belle"s a Doctor of Physics for goodness sake, and completely comfortable with what she did . She does seem to have enjoyed her unusual career. The Porn film industry seems to have become totally acceptable and even mainstream.

Many sports and show business celebrities, many of whom have money, good looks,and some renown, and are lusted over by many of the women on the planet, clearly often favour the services of escorts to the myriad of free opportunities put right in front of them. Hugh Grant features again. But WHY? Perhaps the answer is a simple one. Perhaps it is received wisdom in the world of the well known man that if he wants to go "Off piste " as it were, there is less risk of being found out if he uses an escort than if he went for a freebie random groupie. This way he thinks he buys discretion and confidentiality. Even if this is the case, however, things may be rapidly changing because of the work of investigative journalists (low class ones-thoroughly unrespectable work) and the increasingly tempting and profitable world of "Kiss and tell " for the average Escort girl. It seems there have been some chastening lessons for all of late: If you can"t trust a (High Class) Hooker, who can you trust? By the way, what on earth is Tiger doing for sex these days–my guess is he can"t go to the toilet these days without having a camera shoved up his arse!?

As I said before, The authorities estimate there are approximately 100,000 people working in the prostitution industry in the UK today. Over many centuries, it seems, the authorities have struggled with what to do about it, wavering between banning it altogether (certainly unworkable) to regulating and controlling it, but allowing it.

So why would the average non–celebrity Joe pay for it when there is plenty free? Or is there? And if there isn"t for you, you have problems. Also, the common man doesn"t mind a bit of discretion either. Think about it - having some first hand knowledge myself, I did some research amongst my peer group, and came up with some interesting news and views. This is a bit of a consensus:

"Sex without responsibility. No one gets hurt emotionally. A perfectly reasonable arrangement between two consenting adults.. Get it done and walk away."

Sounds clinical? Well it is. The trouble with extra marital sex (affairs) often is, in the end, that your Mistress wants to marry you and you are always sneaking around. This can lead to all sorts of mess–such as unfaithfulness, constant lies and Divorce. But in the end, many of us (Men and women) are not built for total monogamy for 30-40 years and more. This appears to be a widespread problem. I personally know several Professional men who dabble in Escorts, and it seems its almost becoming fashionable these days to do so. Yes, you know who you are, including several lawyers, businessmen, bankers and accountants. Its not to everyone"s taste, and there is a hint of sleaze I suppose, but at any rate its no one else"s business but their own as long as its discreet. Perhaps it should be legalised and regulated, or at the very least well run parlours should not be victimised. After all, prostitution is almost the oldest profession, and you will never stop it, nor should it be stopped. It is clearly a release valve for many. Driving it underground would be a very bad thing, surely, especially for the girls who need to be protected. Hypocrites shut up!!

All that said, consistently consorting with escorts to the exclusion of other girls doesn"t seem an ideal solution either. I don"t know what the answer is!

On a lighter note, one funny story I heard not so long ago was about a hunger strike amongst some of the men in an Old Folks Home.

The Management couldn"t quite get to what their problem was.

Gradually the truth dawned– there had been a female cleaner who had been "Tossing Off" (some of) the old gents on a regular basis for a (very) small fee. A quid was mentioned! When this was discovered, she was, unsurprisingly I suppose, sacked for "Gross misconduct".

But the beneficiaries of this excellent, unexpected, utterly harmless and very welcome service were not best pleased about her sacking, hence the strike!! It is not recorded if she was re-instated as a result. What a hoot!

CHAPTER EIGHT
THE "70S - A STRIKING PERIOD

The decade saw the last fantasies of our country"s empirical greatness blown away.

It saw the 3 day week under Edward Heath as the miners went on strike for more money.

It saw the first North sea oil discovery by BP and the start of the flow of riches that were to fuel our economy in the eighties and beyond, but before this was to happen we saw the great oil crisis following the 1973 invasion of Israel by several Arab states. High inflation up to 26% followed as higher oil prices and reckless public spending– by Labour, who else– fed into the economy. In 1978 Denis Healey, Labour Chancellor, was forced to borrow from the IMF. Credit cards were also fuelling demand, further driving up prices.

"Buy now pay later "

The "Winter of Discontent" followed in 1978, and the subsequent Vote of "No Confidence " in the Labour Government in Parliament left the door open for Maggie T.

Meanwhile Northern Ireland was a "Tinderbox " and the IRA was at the height of its powers as it switched its attention to Bombings on the mainland for the first time.

The decade opened with a Bang! In 1970 the first 747 "jumbo"passenger jet arrived at Heathrow (Panam Airways). Cheap fuel and these efficient new jets were making cheap worldwide travel available to the masses. Until the 60s, apart from the privileged few, most people holidayed at home. But now the cheap package holiday boom was well underway with Clarksons and Laker Airways–founded 1966- leading the pack. Spain and the Balearics in particular were awash with "Brits " demanding holidays from home– what they wanted was Blackpool with guaranteed sun- so they duly got their "Fish n Chips " and Watney"s Red barrel fare at the expense of the country"s traditional foods, and resorts fell over themselves to make their offering similar to GB seaside holidays. More"s the pity as it ruined the experience for me and many others who were reluctant to return to resorts that changed in this way . We can, however, date the decline in the British holiday resort from the early 70s because of the arrival of the cheap package holiday.

In 1970, The Beatles split up after Paul McCartney went his own way - yes it was that long ago! 40 years! The next year McCartney formed his Band " Wings ".
Band Queen were giving it large..

In 1971 we went "Decimal. The population of the UK in 2010 was 62m. In 1971 it had been 54m.

In that same year, I left London to work in the provinces– to Manchester. Still a Bachelor, I was in need of a change. I had socially and work wise seemed to have reached a kind of a cross-roads, and Alex Lawrie Factors where I was one of two Salesman in the south of England, offered me the job of managing their Manchester sales office. It was a great opportunity so I took a risk and grabbed it with both hands, my only regret being I would not be playing for the Wasps RFC the following season.
I had never visited Manchester city centre but had played rugby against Sale, a suburb, on Wasps Easter tour. I had intended to join Sale once up there but another club intervened and this never happened.
To us southerners, the "North" was a bit of a mystery to say the least–visions of Coronation street housing, mills and chimneys and not much else - but after just a short while I fell in love with it. What struck me straightaway was the friendliness of the people and vibrancy of the Town and its Hinterland . It was full of clubs and great venues hosting a multitude of international music acts such as The Walker Brothers, Four Tops, Shirley Bassey and so on, all of whom I saw live.

George Best was in full Playboy mode, playing for Manchester United, owning clubs, boutiques, hairdressers and drinking himself gradually to disaster. We were always bumping into him around town. It was difficult keeping up but we gave it a go anyway! Having been a distant fan of United for many years, I went to see a game live for the first time.Magical! Besty was unbelievable that day.

After a lonely few summer months first in the Midland hotel– Coronation streets "Albert Tatlock " was a persistent inmate as he actually lived there at the time - and then in a pokey bed-sit, I joined the high flying Wilmslow rugby club, and was invited into a house to live with some fellow players. To everyone"s surprise except theirs, Wilmslow RFC had just beaten Harlequins in the Quarter Final of the National Cup competition. It was a great social club as well as being really successful on the pitch. The club was on the up and their Captain, David Barker,was very persuasive– aided and abetted by the Wilmslow RFC Summer Marquee Ball with its wall-to–wall Birds on display- so I had no hesitation .I went straight into the first team. My life in the north had begun!

Business was good and I was top Salesman in the Country in my second year in the area, even though I managed to find more than enough time to enjoy myself, and I did that with a vengeance not surpassed in my life before or since!

During the next few years the following icons arrived on the scene:

The Stylophone by Rolf Harris. My company financed it and we had free ones all over the house!
Elton John and David Bowie.
Skateboards.
Digital watches and pocket calculators
Trivial Pursuit.
and my favourite, Word Processors–the beginning of the end of the typing pool as we had known it, and the start of us all learning to type. I had the job of persuading the typing pool at Alex Lawrie that these were not a threat to their jobs (they were actually–you don"t see typing pools these days, do you?) but a new and powerful tool to help them. We all type these days don"t we?

In 1975 Microsoft was founded and Star wars the film was released.

 In 1977 Elvis died! Drugs the main cause again. Terrible.

Queens Jubilee with street parties 1977.

In 1979 we were introduced to the Sony Walkman and the age of personal stereo music had arrived.

But the 70s must, first and foremost and regrettably , be regarded as the decade of "Strikes " and Industrial unrest generally.

Our economy was struggling. Conservative Edward Heath P.M– the idiot who took us into the EU on a pretence that it was just a " Common Market "– had tried a financial experiment to get the economy going and it wasn"t working. We ended up, in 1972, with the "3 day week" to save electricity amidst a serious Coal Miners strike. The Postal workers and the Dustmen were also out in support.

 Meanwhile, Heath went sailing.

Wanker.

In 1976, I got married and so did my wife, and Sara was born that same year. Aah!

During that year, one of the longest and driest summers on record– just what you want when you"re pregnant– the water supplies went to record dangerously low levels.

The year went with a "Boom" - it was the year Concorde went into service. A 2100 KPH Supersonic jet. Could do Mach 2.

By now I had been transferred to run an Operations division in Alex Lawrie" s Banbury Head office- into "Line Management". Another great career opportunity grabbed with both hands, although I confess I really missed life in the North, wasn"t over keen on Banbury and its insular farming community, and so determined to return North as soon as possible. In the event, this was not to be for another four years, as the job went so well I couldn"t get away. Promotion followed promotion.

In 1979 the company sent me to Manchester Business School for three months to undertake the " Executive Development Programme " - a sort of concentrated MBA course - which was very hard work, challenging, great fun, and informative. Little did I know that I was destined soon after this to be appointed to the Board to return North and open a branch operations and administration office in Manchester, a new strategy I had been championing for some time. This, for me, was a very big deal indeed! At the relatively young age of 32 I could call myself "Company Director" and the company in question, now a subsidiary of Lloyds Bank, was doing very well indeed!

I had, rather unexpectedly, "arrived"! Not only that, but I could go back North!

So, that year, we returned and went to live in Bramhall, Cheshire.

In the same year, we had the the "Winter of discontent " under P.M James Callaghan with more strikes all leading to the election of my hero– the great "Leaderene" Margaret!!

She would soon sort the all too powerful Unions out. Bring it on Arthur Scargill, you arsehole!

Maggie spent the best part of the 80s kicking the "Woolly pseudo intellectual Socialist nonsense " of the likes of Wilson and Callaghan and company into the long grass, and creating in its place a highly competitive economy. She initiated a neoliberal economic policy of reducing government spending, weakening the power of Trade Unions, stopping tax payer funding of "Lame duck " companies and whole Industries–such as the "Dead duck Industry " coal over which there were terrible strikes ending with the Government winning the day - and promoting economic and trade liberalization. It worked, not without some considerable pain it must be said, but it lead to far more prosperous economic times in the eighties and nineties after the failures of socialist policy in the 60s and 70s. Some lessons are never learned though. Gradually. after they got re-elected in 1997 for the first time in 18 years, the Socialists just went out and made the same mistakes again, only leaving an even bigger deficit this time. The policy of "Tax and spend " always fails in the end.

CHAPTER NINE
LOVE, MARRIAGE, AND CHILDREN

"It is not uncommon for slight acquaintances to get Married, but a couple really have to know each other to get divorced.

Anon

"Me and my Wife were happy for 29 years, then we met."

Les Dawson

Some people have asked me the secret of our long and happy marriage. It"s quite simple really- we take time out to go to a Restaurant twice a week.

She goes Tuesdays, I go Thursdays"

Anon

My Son once got a part in a school play.
  "What"s the part?" I enquired.
"I play a man who"s been Married for 20 years "he told me.
"Don"t worry " I said "One day you"ll get a speaking part."

"Lets go to the Disco after Rugby training - "said John that Wednesday evening .
  "Why not?" I says ."Maybe we"ll meet the girls of our dreams ".
  "Fat chance " said John with a clear lack of optimism.

That said, I wasn"t looking for a wife being a confirmed Bachelor of 30 and having a good life. Just looking for a shag as usual if I"m honest.

I"d never been very good at picking Birds up in Discos–lack of convincing opening gambits and convincing chat lines I think.

"Want to dance?" often elicited the unenthusiastic response:

"No " sometimes "No thanks " sometimes the highly dismissive and dispiriting "No, I"m going to dance with my Friend ". Around the handbags as usual. God, why do they bother to go at all?

It all did nothing for one"s general confidence, of course. We men have had a lot to put up with always having to take the initiative –how about more "Ladies excuse me"s"?

No wonder I hate being rejected and still to this day try to avoid putting myself in that position. Of course, to make ourselves vulnerable sometimes is part of life and missed opportunities result if we don"t.

I"ve not been able to handle rejection ever since a favourite older Cousin rejected a Xmas present I had carefully prepared for her when I was a young Kid. These little things can damage a young sensitive mind.

Anyway, we"re wandering around the place as you do, and suddenly two "Visions of Loveliness " appear right in front of us.

And guess what? John happens to know one of them. Oh joy! We wander over and John addresses the darker one–the others a strawberry blonde. Both Lookers. It turns out it was an old girlfriend from his schooldays. They are sisters. My one looked very Foxy indeed. We chat for a while about nothing in particular, then they go their own way and we continue to wander. A while later, we still had not found anyone better, so I says to John (and why I said it I"ve no idea but I was only joking– many a true word said…..)

"Lets go and talk to the future Mrs Sumner again"

"Yes" they WOULD like a tour round the Dance Floor.Promising. And so it began.

Things moved quickly culminating, from memory, in a quick fumble in the lee of the car park perimeter wall–it was a clear and starry night and the air was sharp keeping me going against the effects of the alcohol, enabling me to be focused on the job in hand I seem to remember. No, she didn"t want to come back to my place that night - presumably wishing to moves things on a little slower that I did - but I left her with her agreement that we would go out the following week. I thought she was probably impressed with my 1971 E Type Jaguar 4.2 Drop Head Coupe which I had recently bought in exchange for my faithful and excellent Datsun 240Z. (She wasn"t as it happens– doesn"t think like that at all)

And so we did. She was undeniably the best looking woman I had ever been with to date. Sex followed sometime over the next few weeks, presumably after she had decided to trust me. I liked that– I don"t want it too easy.I was smitten actually. Her existing Boyfriend was soon dumped and we were an item. I integrated her smoothly into my burgeoning social scene and she became very popular amongst my friends, but Rugby, my main interest, she wasn"t interested in– shame.

We went out regularly- meals with or without friends, parties (lots of in those happy days) We had our special songs-Art Garfunkle comes to mind- and our special restaurants. I was on a Roll in all respects– Career, Socially, Rugby–until I dislocated my elbow that is! Ouch! Sex life getting better all the time. Still as a confirmed Bachelor,I wasn"t looking for a wife, so that"s OK then.

The next few months were, it has to be said, a bit of a blur. Then, all of a sudden I hear the words

"Do you take this woman to be your lawfully Wedded Wife "?
"I do "
"Do you promise to love, honour and obey ...
" Yes" she responded as is the custom.

Of course,"Obey" us is not what women do any more is it? The words we spoke, by the 70s, were way out of date and more in keeping with general practises before the end of the 19th century!

Ok its just possible she "Loved " me, or thought she did, and I her, but "Obey "?

How can you make promises like that? What chance did we think we had of keeping them? And, given the evidence that marriage so often leads to divorce, why do so many couples tread the well worn pathway convinced they have found the elusive magic formula "Till death us do part "? Even at the alter, as we make the vow, is the inherent threat of temptation , although most of us are unaware of it. Our human urge to covet our neighbours spouse haunts us still.

We had a white Mercedes, Church, the Works - I was still a sort of religious believer then although not getting any practise in to be fair. Champagne reception at a nearby Country club no less. The lot. Not a dry eye in the house.

From "Men behaving badly "– I lived with my mate Jeremy and we had a lot of fun as young men tend to do- to marriage in the blink of an eye. He was well pissed off about me getting married and spoiling the party.

I was having to move back down south again to work- not for the last time as you will see later in my story- and it had seemed a good idea to take her as my wife. I guess I got a bit carried away. I discussed it all with a couple of close friends and they thought we were good together and agreed it was a great idea. But I hadn"t really known her long and, in truth, and no offence meant, we didn"t KNOW each other well enough to make as big a decision as marriage. It"s a REALLY BIG decision. We had no idea what we were letting ourselves in for, really we didn"t. We could, after all, have gone down south as an unmarried couple. Nowadays plenty of couples would do that.

So why do we persist in perpetrating this possibly outmoded Institution? Why on earth do we think we can make a success of marriage when so many fail in the end. And why on earth do we spend the deposit for a small house on one day celebrating it? The organisation, the stress, the expense. Who benefits from this ritual extravaganza? That said, I must say I do like a good wedding- my daughters in Italy was FANTASTIC fun, and she"s still happily married in so far as one can judge. Good girl! Anyway, the enjoyment of the actual event aside, sorry to be a cynic, but why do we keep saying "I do " when so many people are getting divorced or just unhappily married and dogging it out "For the sake of the Kids " or just hanging onto each other like they would otherwise drown? I wonder how many people in that church when we married went on to have happy marriages? How many of them were already getting jiggy with other peoples wives , having affairs? I could name some of them then and more of them now.

Forever is a very long time. People change. In my view, even if you arrive at the steps of the church harbouring serious doubts-which IS very late I agree, as all the arrangements have been made and everyone"s arrived- be prepared to stop it there and then. Not easy, but better than the alternatives. Expensive to cancel things at that point but MUCH more expensive to get out of it later. The reality is, in fact, that less and less couples are getting Wed.

But I had not a moments doubt about the whole thing until,….well, until the Honeymoon actually. After all, I was one of the last of my old friends to get married, I was 29 and that seemed old enough–it wasn"t. I wasn"t ready. Really wasn"t. For me, at a guesstimate, 40 would have been a better age to get married as it turned out. More mature, knowing ones own mind, and settled by then.

So, a sense of foreboding came over me. What had I done? Was it some sort of mistake or just initial doubts?

Had I married because it seemed like the right time, no more than that? No it was more than that, but how final marriage seems once you"re in it! Increasingly I felt like a Bear caught in a trap.

Our honeymoon– a ski trip, the first for both of us and in Scotland of all places to choose(A client of mine at the time had INSISTED it was great there). I fell on my first day and, having pulled knee ligaments, couldn"t ski again. So we just went for long walks every day, in my case hobbling. The snow was poor anyway. It was a pretty Crap trip really, and not a good start. So much for "Confirmed Bachelorhood ". Swept away in a moment.

It had been a year since we met– a YEAR!! Good God that"s no time at all, what was I thinking? What was SHE thinking?

My advice concerning marriage ? Well, these days we really don"t need to get married at all, and many do not. However, should you chose to do so, REALLY ensure you know your mind, and give your relationship time to blossom before you take this enormous step. Are you friends as well as lovers? Do you talk? Do you have things other than Sex in common? Could you envisage ever wanting another woman at any time in the future? Someone once said:

"You shouldn"t marry someone you can live with, you should marry someone you can"t live without."

Good advice that. If all this is the case, then fine, go for it. Don"t get me wrong- I"m not against marriage as such and my Missus is not only beautiful– even now- but smart too and a good woman who everyone likes probably more than they like me.. I merely ask the question. Some marriages truly do work long term, but these days the minority. In our day marriage was something that was not given the consideration it is now, and was very much the expected "Norm" at some point before reaching 30. But in the end we just get carried away with it all– making the arrangements and all that. Any doubts are cast aside.

Looking back, the truth is I"m not sure I was ever built for marriage. At the very least I believe I got married too young at a time when I didn"t understand the nature of love or,indeed, marriage and the nature of the commitment. I was basically unfit at the time for either marriage or fatherhood, and our Sara came quickly as it turned out. Mind you I couldn"t have done without having the kids. I really do love my kids.They are the best in the world, these particular children. We are so lucky. You probably feel exactly the same way about yours. Kids ARE forever. I regard ours as a real achievement, as I do the fact that I have been married for 35 years. We still love them, they still love us. They are balanced and well adjusted, happy and positive. They don"t do drugs and …..

Anyway, I"m getting ahead of myself. It didn"t take long for her to fall pregnant. Strange how some couples who are REALLY trying hard have such a problem.Doesn"t seem fair. It happened only two months after the Wedding. We had never discussed having kids and she had always been on the Pill therefore no issues.(literally and metaphorically, as it were). Time on our own without distractions to get to know each other would have been better. Kids are wonderful but not for everybody and both Partners need to discuss all implications, whether or not to have them at all, timing etc and be in full agreement.

Anyway, there were no regrets on my part- still aren"t- and out came the Champagne. I was going to be a Father.

We had no idea what we were letting ourselves in for! Nobody warns you! There were no manuals. O.k there are, but I never read any of them, put it that way! I went to the birth like all good modern men -on the day it was freezing brass monkeys and couldn"t at once get into the car to go to the hospital having been summonsed."Its time ". Lock frozen. "Don"t panic "- I had the presence of mind to boil a kettle and I was away and arrived on time-just. Odd thing the placenta- the doctor said our daughter"s was an "Interesting and unusual specimen". Can"t remember why. Sara was (and is) lovely of course and I immediately loved this little bundle of blood, skin, wrinkles, orifices and noise. Funny that. Four years later we had a second–The boy Adam this time. Having kids was great and I loved them so much-still do of course. Not a day goes past without you worrying about them, of course. They are so "Caring", always ringing up and finding out how we are, much more so than I did with my Parents, to whom I went for months on end without speaking, not because we"d had a row, but because no-one could be bothered to pick up the phone.

CHAPTER TEN
THE PROBLEM WITH MARRIAGE

"The chief reason why marriage is rarely a success is that its contracted while the Partners are insane "

Joseph Collins– Writer

Sometimes I wonder if men and women really suit each other. Perhaps they should live next door and just visit now and then

Katherine Hepburn -Actress

"Instead of getting married, why not just find someone you don"t like and buy them a House-it might turn out to be cheaper in the long run"

Anon

Of course its possible to love a human being if you don"t know them too well.

Charles Bukowski - US Poet and Author

Before we start let me assure you I love my Wife and she loves me, OK! Otherwise, why would we still be married?

Of course, the Institution of marriage such as we practise it these days hasn"t always been on the agenda in life.

Marriage, as we know it in our Western civilization today, has a long history with roots in several very different ancient cultures, of which the Roman, Hebrew, and Germanic are the most important, and has taken different forms. Western marriage has further been shaped by the doctrines and policies of the medieval Christian church, the demands of the Protestant Reformation, and the social impact of the Industrial Revolution. There was a period of time during the Roman Republic when the marriage ceremony was a solemn religious ordinance. Later, however, religion fell into contempt and marriage became virtually a civil contract. The growth of Christianity then started to reverse this. Again, early in Roman history, a husband had considerable power over his wife and children, whom he could punish, sell, or even kill as he saw fit. However, eventually women came to enjoy a better legal position and gained more and more control over their lives and property. Thus, in later Roman Imperial times husband and wife began to approach marriage as equals. Yet it seems that there was a subsequent decline in marriage and birth rates. Polygamy, men having multiple wives at once, is one of the most common marital arrangements represented in the Hebrew Bible, yet scholars doubt that it was common among average Israelites because of the wealth needed to practice it. As we know, it was practiced by some Mormons (Brigham Young"s Latter Day Saint movement based on Utah and Salt lake city the prime example) in the USA at one stage in their history from the 1830s onwards, but this is largely no longer the case. I think I could make a case for polygamy, but I don"t think I would find much support at home! As long ago as the 17th century many couples used formal betrothal as an excuse to move in together leading to much pre-marital pregnancy. From the 1690s through to the nineteenth century, married women in England had no legal standing. Even before that, wife sale was common in rural and small town England. In 1553 Thomas Snowdel, Clergyman, sold his wife to a butcher after Queen Mary 1 pronounced that all priests who had married during short initial period of Protestantism under her father Henry V111, should be thrown out of their livings. Wives were often sold through small ads in newspapers or exchanged for goods such as an Oxen! To divorce his wife, a husband could present her with a rope around her neck in a public sale to another man.

Marriage by force or capture goes back to primitive culture when tribal groups were routinely hostile to each other. At that time marriages were "consummated" as the groom captured a desirable woman in the process of conquering and pillaging a rival tribe. The honeymoon is a relic of the days of marriage by capture. Frequently the tribe from which a warrior stole a bride would come looking for her, and it was necessary for the warrior and his new wife to go into hiding to avoid being discovered. "Marriage by Purchase" or contract - going back to Anglo-Saxon times - probably evolved from marriage by force. Exchange, outright sale, service, child betrothal, and gift giving were the primary methods for the purchase/contract marriage. The bride was first stolen, and later compensation was provided to her family or tribe to escape their retribution. The custom of purchasing a wife began with the desire to placate enraged parents, and also to avoid tribal warfare that might result if such compensation were not forthcoming. In the earliest stages of "Marriage by Purchase", an exchange was made instead of a price being paid. Imagine that a would-be bridegroom, having recently stolen his bride away from her family, is overtaken by her angry family and is ordered to pay for her. Unable to do so, he offers instead to exchange his own sister, his livestock, or his land for her. In this way he is able to not only save his own life, but able to keep his freedom and new wife as well. The price would be determined by rank, with a virgin worth rather more than a widow for example. If a man found out his new wife did not match the description, then he could get his money back! Many fathers were willing to turn a buck for selling a daughter. But eventually King Cnut ("Canute") enacted a law in the 11th century stating no woman could be forced to marry against her will in an attempt to stop the practise. However, Under Cnut, any adulteress had her ears and nose cut off! It seems that, anagrammatically speaking at least, Cnut was a bit if a Cunt after all.

Then there were Fleet marriages A "Fleet" Marriage is the best-known example of an irregular or a clandestine marriage taking place in England before the Marriage act came into force on March 25, 1754. Specifically, it was one which took place in London"s Fleet prison(in Fleet street, London) or its environs during the 17th and, especially, the early 18th century. Technically, under English law a marriage could be recognized as valid if each spouse had simply expressed (to each other) an unconditional consent to their marriage. But these "common law" marriages were the exception. Nearly all marriages in England, including the "irregular" and "clandestine" ones, were performed by ordained clergy. The privately owned prison soon realized they could make money by employing prisoner clergymen to take (clandestine) wedding ceremonies. That is to say where there was an element of secrecy required , for example, bigamy or under age marriages. In the early 18th century some 4000 Fleet weddings per year were being enacted there or in its environs . By 1740 this figure had risen to some 6500– about half the marriages in London. Drunken clergymen and their Agents would tout for business up and down The Street and Ludgate Hill trying to persuade equally drunken people to get married. That said, while some of the Fleet marriages were for criminal or fraudulent purposes, the great majority of the couples marrying there did so with the aim of making a normal lasting union.

When we look at the marriage customs of our ancestors, we discover some other striking facts. For example, for the most of Western history, marriage was not a mere personal matter concerning only husband and wife, but rather the business of their two families which brought them together, such as we still find in some Asian and other cultures. Many marriages, therefore, were arranged. Moreover, the wife usually had rather fewer rights than her husband and was expected to be subservient to him. To a considerable extent, marriage was also an economic arrangement. There was little room for romantic love, and even simple affection was not considered essential. Procreation and cooperation were the main marital duties. Um!

On the other hand, it may surprise many modern couples to learn that in earlier times divorce was often easily granted. Here again, men usually had the advantage when they could simply dismiss their wives, but in many instances women could also sue for divorce. In ancient Rome couples could even divorce each other by mutual agreement, a possibility that has not yet returned to all European countries.

Monogamy is expected by 95 % of couples when they first enter marriage, yet a survey by the "Social and economic sciences research centre at Washington state university " of sexually active Seattle residents aged 18-39 found that "27% of men and 18% of women reported that during their most recent sexual relationship they had sex with one other partner." Another statistic suggests that 10% of children in Britain don"t belong to the men they are supposed to! In Scandinavia I believe this ratio goes up to 15% plus, at least it does according to Scandinavian crime writer Jo Nesbo!!

And so are we entirely suitable for monogamy anyway? Even my Brother, who didn"t seem the type, started an affair with his PA at his work. He ended up marrying her and divorcing his wife of 10 years or so who, after years of trying and treatment, had just delivered, to everyone"s surprise and delight, two Boys, back to back. Heart-breaking for her. Our Mother was not best pleased– she loved Kim– and said if anyone was going to do that sort of thing it would be me. Charming! Personally, I make no judgements about this matter one way or the other.

The papers are always full of celebrities cheating on their wives/ husbands. Tiger Woods, John Terry, Harold Pinter and even the sweet Lady Antonia Fraser, Warren Beatty and many, many more. The tendency is,of course, not confined to Celebrities. Life"s statistics seem to make a mockery of our cultural dedication to monogamy. Midlife marriage break-up is everywhere as people evaluate their lives even in their 50s and 60s which they never used to do. And its not just infidelity that"s leading to splits– just boredom or growing incompatibility, changing mutual interests or whatever. In the days of us Baby Boomer generation"s parents, the tendency was to stay together, partly because they couldn"t afford to be apart and anyway, in those days, life expectancy wasn"t nearly so long, and therefore the time span of the commitment was so much shorter. In Victorian times, because of early death, the average marriage lasted only 15 years!

Women, in particular, thought very differently in those days. Nowadays more women are independent minded and, crucially, often but clearly not always, financially independent and can make a life choice of their own.

Baby Boomers generally are, it seems to me, different from previous generations.Their life expectancy is longer, they are better educated, wealthier and aspirations are generally much higher. If they are unhappy over a long period they just won"t stand for it and will change it, it seems. Many, I would say most , of our married friends and acquaintances over the years have indeed split up. Long term marriage is, it seems, very difficult indeed to sustain. Also, the Internet has made it easier for older people to find a new partner.

One view regarding sex outside marriage is that:

"This is normal behaviour for a mammal, who revert to primal instincts. Its nurture not nature that makes us monogamous".

It is said by scientists that men are, in fact, "Biologically disposed to spread their seed ". In other words we can"t help ourselves boys. That explains it then! This doesn"t, of course explain predatory (sexually) married women, many of whom (alright some of whom) over the years have propositioned me albeit not always successfully I"m proud to say. In reality things go on and blind eyes are turned. Long term monogamous relationships can be hard, even dull, certainly routine, and need working at. Over time, the physical thing almost inevitably becomes gradually less exciting, and I suppose we want more out of relationships than is reasonable, but do we expect too much? Are not our expectations too high? So just HOW do you keep the relationship fresh and positive? Well don"t ask me!

A friend of mine calls his wife the "EPO " (Entertainment Prevention Officer) which is perhaps slightly unfair, but you get the gist.

THE DIFFERENCES BETWEEN MEN AND WOMEN

Of course we men are quite different from women in many ways.

One of the biggest differences between Men and Women, my research indicates, is how they cope with stress.

For example, when I came home from work each night tired out, all I wanted to do was play with the kids for a bit, flop in front of the TV and not have to think. To escape the rigours of work . I didn"t want to talk. I daresay I seemed distant. What my wife wanted to do was to unburden herself from her problems of the day by talking about them. This is a common problem. Hence, I suppose, the feeling amongst men that women talk too much. I always tended to want to solve my own problems, or the family problems, on my own. It"s a natural thing for men, but one tends to brood about them and withdraw into ones shell. This clearly leads to less communication and the wife doesn"t get the attention she craves and, lets face it, deserves. The wife begins to resent all this, feels she is being ignored and things build up. Tension is created in the home. If my wife had a problem, I would give her what I regarded as a top solution and get back into my shell. I realise now this is not what she wanted at all– she wanted to TALK! I must admit looking back, I could often be remarkably dismissive of my wife"s issues– which often seemed to me rather trivial compared to work matters - and it makes me cringe, in retrospect, to think of it. I had often, and rather unreasonably, threatened to take my ball away every time when there was a major row going on. This must have driven her nuts. On the other side, she was always trying to improve my behaviour–to change me. Talking to friends over the years, it turns out most women want to do that with their husbands or their partners for that matter, and it often concerns nothing more important than the household chores. This really can piss men off!

We know, of course, that men don"t like to be "Nagged". Research tells me, historically, it has only been the women who have been "Naggers " from the Scandinavian "To gnaw, pick, or nibble at something". Its not something men usually do. Interestingly, and I swear to you this is true, until the early 19th century, english and european law allowed for a husband to complain to a magistrate about his wife"s "nagging" or "scolding". If his case was proved, the wife would be sentenced to the "Ducking Stool". This was additionally used to punish Prostitutes, witches and minor offenders. It, of course, involved being strapped to a seat and ducked in a local pond or river as many times as seemed to the Magistrate to fit the seriousness, or otherwise, of the offence. Some of the worst offenders were also paraded around town in an iron mask. The ducking practise came to an end in 1809, and I"m not advocating a comeback - honest - but of course nagging rarely works on us men, sometimes having the opposite effect and other times destroying the relationship completely.

> *"The only time a woman really succeeds in changing a man*
> *is when he"s a baby"*
>
> *Natalie Wood*

In other words: "A woman marries a man expecting he will change for the better but he doesn"t, and a man marries a woman expecting she won"t change, but she does (for the worse)!"

So:
He doesn"t listen

She doesn"t acknowledge his role and corrects his behaviour as if he were a child (He is, but that"s not the point!) This is a bad move– women should almost never waste their time trying to "Improve " their man. It will be resented. A man needs to be accepted even if he isn"t perfect (I KNOW I"m Not)

He doesn"t understand why she won"t accept him as he is, so he repeats the behaviour!

He needs to be trusted and accepted as the Breadwinner.

She needs to feel he cares for her. To feel loved and cherished.

She doesn"t like it when he forgets to do the things she asks.

He doesn"t understand her viewpoint.

He should NOT argue with her "Feelings " and her opinions. They are real, even if he can"t understand WHY she feels that way.

She should understand he"s NOT a mind-reader! He does NOT know what she is feeling nor what she wants him to DO!

Lets face it Boys, we do make mistakes so lets hold our hands up!

But in my opinion, at the end of the day, a man should forget his mistakes– there"s no point in two people remembering the same thing!

There are other fundamental problems between the sexes, due to basic differences in their makeup. For instance,men can only do one thing at a time. Apparently, they have a thinner "corpus callosum "chord than women– the chord that connects the left and right brain hemispheres . This obliges men to concentrate fully on the job in hand and when their woman speaks they often cannot hear them. The woman thinks we are ignoring her of course as they can multi task so, for example, can hear a man speak when they are reading and will respond. They assume men can do this too. Women don"t know about the mans inherent limitation, but would be well advised to give their man only one job at a time if they want a stress free life.

Its all very complicated. No wonder relationships break down. Familiarity does seem to breed contempt as often or not- we get to know too many of the downsides about our partners I suppose. A negative history builds up over time which can be re-cycled. Of course, it eventually becomes clear that we are fundamentally different from each other as people , and we don"t understand each other at all.

It seems that the old marriage model is breaking down after years of relative success, and many young people are not keen to get involved with it. For all its benefits and joys, marriage is a compromise and involves, amongst other things, restraint, and inevitably restricts the individual for the good of the marriage.One has other people to consider and therefore some of the available fruits of life must be eschewed for the common good. Marriage becomes a "comfort zone" or even a "prison cell", in which we are not necessarily able to express ourselves as freely as we would like. For an essentially expressive and selfish person such as myself, this can be difficult, even impossible, over a long period of time.

So how could or should marriage be adjusted for the modern age?

Perhaps set an initial time or age limit, at which point one or both can decide to go their separate ways without all the lawyers making a fortune?

Lifelong monogamy, then, seems to be a romantic notion more than a practical outcome in many cases. All in all, lets face it, many, many married people are at it!

History tells us the marriage model has moved on before and it will do so, gradually I dare say, again.

My wife and I have had some BIG arguments over the years. We could really hurt each other– say dreadful things. We could each wind the other up in seconds by tearing the scabs off old wounds. Replaying arguments long since past but not resolved. Sometimes we would have a "Cold War " when we just wouldn"t speak for days on end. That"s not good, but nowadays someone usually breaks the Ice within a few hours and the other will acquiesce. We can still lock horns and then it becomes a battle of wills, but it is usually quickly over."Sorry " is eventually said, and is important, but perhaps on occasion resentment lingers and simmers only to be re-cycled at some future point.

Someone once said:

" In marriage, one can chose to be right or one can chose to be happy, but usually not both. "

This seems to sum things up for me.

But in the old days, neither of us seemed to be able to be big enough to end the war and talk about it. In truth, and ironically, we NEVER seemed to have an argument about anything important. About the Kids - the Kids schooling for example, never a crossed word. Never argued about sex, not that I recall anyway. Nor about housekeeping- at least not until much later in life. We just seemed to get on each others tits! And neither understood WHY! Well at least I didn"t.

Anyway, as time went by we seemed to be drifting and, to my mind, our marriage seemed to be struggling. In truth we were probably having no more problems than many other married couples with young children but we were having a lot of rows and just didn"t seem to be getting on with each other at all well. I personally think that when the kids arrive is the most dangerous time for a relationship, which can go either way. All, or at least most, of that love and affection the woman felt for the man– and he felt from her- is now going to be transferred to the kid/s!! This tends to be noticed by the man and can lead to feelings of rejection and separateness to add to other feelings of being trapped. So after about seven years of marriage and out of the blue, I suggested a separation. I was going back to London to start this new job so it seemed an apposite moment. She readily agreed. Too readily, I suppose, and that made me more determined at that time. Actually, when we came to explain our decision to family, friends and Solicitors as to WHY we wanted to separate, we couldn"t seem to list any truly convincing reasons at all. The one I felt sorry for was my daughter who, at 8 years of age, was old enough to feel some of the pain. I felt awful for her. My son at 4 was far too young to know what was going on I think, so may not have been affected by what happened at that time. Still, we went ahead with it, and started proceedings through Lawyers - in the end the only "Winners " when it comes to marital breakdown.

I had to work really hard when I got to London, and any sort of social life wasn"t possible, partly because I didn"t know many people down there any more and was lonely really. Many of my old mates were spread to the four corners of the earth and I had no way of seeing them on a regular basis. What I really needed was a couple of regular drinking buddies and a girlfriend but where to find ? I hadn"t joined any clubs– I hadn"t had time. In retrospect I should have joined the local rugby club but, at the time, I thought I was finished with rugby! How wrong can one be, as I ended up taking it up again four years later!

Ever been lonely? I was certainly missing my family and friends but ploughed on anyway. I hadn"t really ever liked living alone as a bachelor. So I drank- a lot. Actually, I tried to drink my way through it all really, and ate fast food and became a bit dishevelled. The house was always a mess. No woman to look after me you see and I wasn"t used to all that washing, ironing and washing up and keeping the house tidy and I was working really hard. And I was missing the kids– I knew I would, but I was missing them much more than I had thought I would . It was painful. Really painful. I was hurting inside, but it was a bed of my own making and I had to lie in it. And I was so lonely. Life seemed endless work and no play, even though I did have one or two isolated unsuccessful "Dates ". The answer to my lack of female company, indeed company of any kind apart from business people at work and a few nights out with old friends Paul and Sooty, arrived courtesy an old school friend in a very strange and unpredictable way. All those of a nervous disposition look away NOW.

I was throwing a party in Richmond, Surrey, where my new house was located, for old friends. They came from all over. Several from my old southern Rugby Club, the Old Citizens. Amongst the party goers was my oldest school friend Ginger–remember him- who turned up with his Mistress and wow- even before she got over my threshold, immediate sparks between us began to fly. She was strikingly beautiful with neat auburn hair, pert breasts, slim. 5"7" or so at a guess. Gorgeous. Sexy as hell and all over me. It was electric. We danced all night ignoring everyone else it seemed and we both got more and more pissed. I don"t know about her, but I could hardly stand up when, about 2 am in the morning, she says " you had better show me around your lovely house then ". Then she went for me big-time. How could I say no, even if it had occurred to me? My mate was nowhere to be seen. As it subsequently turned out he had fallen into one of the beds upstairs completely bombed! But here I was -well pissed and, well defenceless. This is not an excuse for my behaviour which was shabby to say the least. Ten minutes later she is all over me and we are shagging each others brains out in my bed. And she was good.Very good. She absolutely loved sex and had made the move on me, but she was one of my best and oldest Mate"s Birds right? I had broken the code and was not proud of it. Never shag your mates " Bird". I never had before. Then disaster. Some time during the night my bedroom door opened–it was Ginger. He took one look at the scene in front of him and, saying nothing, fled out the door, out of the house , got in his car and went home.To Devon from Richmond, at 4 pm in the morning after drinking God knows how much. He told me later he eventually and very illegally pulled up on the hard shoulder of the M5 somewhere near Exeter and, exhausted, fell asleep. He had, unhappily, forgotten to pull on the handbrake, and woke up some time later in the outside fast lane whence the car had drifted backwards to all on its own! Unbelievable! The mind boggles about how he managed to survive the experience but he did.

You"ll never get what happened next. He forgave me. He rang me a few days later.

" We"ve been friends for ever Brian. She"s not worth giving that up for and the irony of the situation hasn"t escaped me ".

You see, he was being unfaithful to his Wife, I was separated from mine, and had been for more than a year.

We had become friends at the age of 11 in class O2B at the City of London school. We played in the same rugby team at school then at the Old Boys for a number of years until I joined Blackheath Rugby Club. We had schooled together, holidayed together, partied together, played Rugby together, lost our best friends in that car accident together, and loved and lost together. His old man was a wealthy Solicitor and when Ginger was 21, his Dad helped him fund the creation of a young peoples activity centre in Devon near historic Kingsbridge, nestling in the picturesque Aune Valley. What a great area it is. I love going down there even now. He had bought a wonderful old Manor House complete with ramparts, and converted the outbuildings to suitable accommodation.He ran Courses there for parties of school kids and University students for many years. You know the sort of thing- sailing, orienteering, canoeing, field studies. For years before and after the incident described above we would often go down with our kids, and always had a wonderful time in spite of his well known disorganisation skills. He was always disappearing and the cry often went out:

"Where"s Ginger"?

This is the same man that took 2 days servicing his speedboat prior to that Pirate Radio station jaunt, then forgot to put oil in the outboard leading to engine blow up. Complex man was Ginger. His wife eventually left him in the early 80s having taken up with an itinerant New Zealander who proceeded to whisk her and Ginger"s kids off to NZ. Now that"s unkind, and he never really got over it, as he had to spend the next 15 to 20 years travelling to the other side of the world to see them once a year at the most. Poor sod! I felt for him, but he, like me, was hardly "New Man ". Years later, not long ago actually, and very sadly, he died of a terrible cancer . He is much missed. Alarmingly, another friend from our class at school died of the same cancer, Oesophageal, 6 months later. Colonel "Spew "Jones. What sort of a co-incidence can that be? Am I next?

As it happens, the young lady in question and I went out for some months. She had her own business, was unmarried, and lived just outside Kingsbridge in a pretty village.I often went for weekends. After all I was separated and needed female companionship very badly. She was great– she really looked after me. We talked about her coming to London to live but my mind was focussing elsewhere and I eventually felt I had to dump her– she hadn"t a clue it was coming and I felt awful about it at the time and afterwards . We had got on really great together. You see, I had had an attack of divorce jitters and decided, against the odds, to try and repair my almost irreparable marriage. In fact I was having a "Breakdown " with the worry of it all. She had to go. Or did she? For a while, I changed my mind again. Back and forth I went in my decision.Should I try to repair my broken marriage or not?I couldn"t decide and I couldn"t sleep either. And I was becoming more and more ill. More and more depressed as time was going by.

Then I finally made my mind up and finished with her for the last time. Of course, this is often the lot of the Mistress. Husbands, when it comes to it, and as often as not, don"t leave their wife and children. It was then that I really did fall apart- see "Prologue" - and ended up in the Priory Hospital.

CHAPTER ELEVEN
THE ACTOR

"Acting is the most minor of gifts- after all, Shirley temple could do it when she was four"

Katherine Hepburn

Why do we feel embarrassed,impatient, ill–at–ease, assembled like Amateur Actors who have not been assigned their parts"

TS Elliott

"Learn your lines and don"t bump into the furniture"

Spencer Tracy

One of my Passions nowadays is Amateur theatre. This has gradually crept up on me over a long period of time.

"The Mobberley players are a man short for a big part in their next production- "A Bedroom Farce" by Alan Aykborn"

announced my wife one day, many years ago.

"So what"s that to do with me?" I enquired naively.

"I said you would do it " she says.

"What makes you think I"ll do it, that I"ll be any good or even that they will have me? " I said , hoping they wouldn"t have me. I hadn"t acted since my school days 20 years before, and not a great deal back then.

" Because they are desperate " she continued.

"What"s the part? " I asked

""Malcolm " she continued. "He makes a cabinet and it falls apart at the end and its supposed to be very funny. It sounds like the part"s tailor made for you ". Charming.

And so , some twenty years ago, my post school days amateur acting career began in this rather unpromising fashion. They DID have me, I did accept for some reason, and I duly went along to rehearsals. But why did I do it? I really wasn"t sure I should or even that I could. Because it seemed a worthwhile challenge I suppose - I feel in life its generally a good thing to stretch oneself and see what happens. This was one of those moments when one has the opportunity to step forward and take a risk. Get out of ones "Comfort Zone ". Make oneself vulnerable. Nowhere much more vulnerable than on a stage in front of hundreds of critical theatre goers including the ultimate Critics- friends and family. Anyway, I had always harboured a bit of a desire to act, and was aware of some, but as it turned out not all, of the pitfalls. Easy to say "No" but perhaps better to say "Yes".

Like when I was in Cairns, Australia with my wife and some friends, and all down the high street were shops offering sky diving. Now I had always said there was no way I would EVER jump out of a plane–no way Jose.

But my Son had passed through Cairns some years before on his post Uni back- packing odyssey, and he had done it. Much to his mothers concern. Actually, she didn"t find out until long after he was safely back in England , so any concern was entirely mis-timed so much too late. Naturally, anything he can do, I can do, so I booked in for the following morning. 8 Am. I report back to the Missus what I have done.

"You stupid Man " she says "You"ll kill yourself. Go back at once and cancel it".

"Look " I said, "If I die, I die ", somewhat fatalistically.

" Adams done it, so I"m going to ".

" Yes but he"s not a stupid old man " (I was approaching 60)
Charming.

However, once I"d told her there was a A$lm insurance in place for any death as a result, she, rather suspiciously I thought at the time, seemed to calm down- even acquiesce. (actually, there wasn"t such an insurance in place) The Instructor was a Cool Aussie who had been there before– about 2000 times, he revealed.

"Without once killing yourself?" I enquired somewhat suspiciously.

"" No, not once " he replied.

Well, what were the chances of my coming back alive? Getting better all the time, I thought. I did the jump having spent all night basically and literally shitting myself, and, like my son, I have the video to prove it. My wife even came to watch. You don"t think she was hoping......? Anyway, it was fantastic.

Acting is like jumping out of a plane but without a parachute.

I read the script. Rehearsals start and I meet my stage " Wife " for the first time. Bit of a "Munter" if I"m honest, but its only pretend. I check in the script to see if I have to kiss her. I don"t– Good! We do the first read through. It goes OK. It seems quite an amusing part. No problems so far.

"You must have your lines learnt in a month " explains the Director and

" Only eight weeks to curtain up. "

Oh Shit, I thought, that"s not long.That"s when the real pressure started. When it always starts. Um, I thought, far too many words to remember. Fewer may have been better as a first effort, but eventually I sort of learnt them but wasn"t sure how I would go under pressure, in performance. "It"ll be alright on the night" only applies if you, and the rest of the cast for that matter, have prepared VERY thoroughly. The old adage "Fail to prepare, then prepare to Fail " applies very much to the Theatre, be it amateur or professional.

On the first night "Malcolm " and his stage missus are lying in bed in the dark as the curtain rises.I was cacking myself. Half my staff from work were in the front row, just waiting for me to fail! The fat internal auditor was right there in my face, taking up two seats he was so vast,and he seemed to be thinking:

"Ok Boss, lets see what you got and you better be good!"

I had no idea whether I would be any good, or even whether I would be able to remember all or indeed any of my lines when called upon to do so. I have often been asked since, during rehearsals for other productions, whether I had learnt my lines yet. Paraphrasing Eric Morecambe , I always reply:

"Yes, I remember my lines, but not necessarily in the right order".

I eventually figured for myself that authors wrote those particular words because they wanted to hear THOSE words spoken in performance of their play, so I knew making your own words up was to be avoided. Of course, when all else fails, approximating the gist (paraphrasing) may well be all that"s left and DISTINCTLY preferable to saying nothing on stage ("Drying"). "Bedroom Farce " is a comedy, but I didn"t want people laughing at ME, I wanted them to laugh at my character, Malcolm, and when they are supposed to. So I took it all quite seriously.

"Acting comedy is the most difficult form of acting",

I had read somewhere, and I had no idea at all what I was doing. None.. oh Shit. I kept expecting the Director to say

" Don"t just do something- stand there!" (Sam Goldwyn"s classic line to a rather poor and raw actress he was directing).

What HAD I let myself in for? When it was over, everyone agreed it had gone quite well. Even my friends and my staff said I was OK. They all seemed surprised. I know I was.

Acting and the "Arts " generally were considered a bit sissy for a rugby player, even though one of our flankers at the Old citizens had been in the famous "Frank and Peggy Spencer " Ballroom Dance team that used to be on Telly in the 60s and 70s, and we didn"t consider him a sissy . He was pretty "Hard ". As was actor / rugby player Richard Burton though even he was also considered a bit soft by his Mates in his early days of trying to be an actor. However, the fact he was a fellow rugby player gave me confidence. In many ways, however, I think its quite manly, and who doesn"t want to be James Bond or something?. Times have changed anyway. Most people readily admit they would be too scared to do it. Most of my mates say they wouldn"t do it "For all the Tea in China" and seem to respect me for having a go, even allowing slip-ups.

One of the most frightening experiences in life I have ever had was what the acting profession calls the "Dry "particularly when, for no apparent reason, you forget a cue or a line that, throughout weeks and months of rehearsals you never, ever, forgot. In companies without "Prompts" – a bit like Trapeze artists without a harness- you are left all alone exposed in the middle of the stage to shit yourself until a fellow actor comes to the rescue by winging it until harmony is restored and you remember where you are supposed to be in the script. I know because I have been in a production without a "Prompt". In "Bedroom Farce", I was cruising along full of confidence as everything was going really well, then, at some point during the scene where Malcolm is about to see his labours turn to dust when his cabinet collapses, it happened. I don"t realise its my line next and it all goes quiet. Everyone on the stage starts looking at everyone else and the Prompt has clearly dozed off, or gone home or something. Then she says the cue and I STILL don"t realise its my line. She says it again, LOUDER this time at which point I get it, and we"re off again with no further mishaps. That night at least. But it was my only slip of the week as it turned out!. Why it should happen on a line you really know very well I don"t understand , but it can and has happened to me at various points during all of the plays I have ever done, fortunately not every night and rarely the same line. That"s what is so frightening about it. And I can tell you it concentrates the mind. One of my worst moments was during the first night of Agatha Christies "Witness for the Prosecution" with the Woodford players, a murder drama, where I had my first lead role, and was on stage for the best part of 2 hours with huge amounts of dialogue. I played the very grand Sir Wilfred Robarts, Counsel for the Defence, a part I had won against my will and more about which later. Having explained to the Director "I wasn"t very experienced" and had "No Chance " of carrying it off. My previous part, the first for 20 years, was a year before in Bristol when I played the rather pompous Sir William Lucas in "Pride and Prejudice" which was an excellent, if small, part ideal for me for obvious reasons. Actually, I have played no less than three " Knights of the Realm " in my relatively short acting career! Typecast already!

Anyway,
"Who are the Woodford players "
I had asked my wife some months before I was eventually cast as Sir Wilfred?

"No idea, but if neither of us has heard of them , their publicity machine is clearly not one of their strong suits " she said.

"Lets hope acting and direction IS then " I said.

So I went along and as it happened they were, that very night, holding auditions for their next play. I was asked to join in and pick a couple of parts to read from several piles on the side which I did. I chose two small ones, not wishing to be presumptuous. I had ½ hour to read them through before facing the Casting Committee. Long enough. It came to my turn to read- which did go quite well I have to say- and was about to go when the Chairman and the Director asked me to read another part, which turned out to be the Lead role! The notes indicated this part "Carries the bulk of the dialogue". My heart started to beat very fast. So I read as requested and off I went home. Again, I felt it went well, but their response was:

"We"ll let you know ", somewhat dismissively I thought at the time. Clearly I was not going to get it. Thank God for that! However, amazingly, three days later, I get an Email which said words to the effect I had indeed been offered the Lead in the play, "Witness for the Prosecution ". Sir Wilfred Robarts QC was memorably played, in a celebrated 1930s film, by Charles Laughton, and I"m no Charles Laughton of course ! I was truly gob smacked. It seemed like a joke. I was clearly the wrong man for the job: I had done precisely three plays in 40 years at various Societies, with only one role that could be considered in any way major (Malcolm). I had NEVER before had a Leading Man role. Or a Leading Lady role for that matter! There was the small matter of a huge number of lines to learn. They didn"t know me from "Adam " and couldn"t really have had any idea of my character, reliability or anything . But they were experienced–the Chairwoman turns out to be an Ex Pro director– and they thought they saw something. God only knows what. I tried to persuade them to drop me. They insisted I would be fine. How brave of them! I checked that they weren"t a "Mickey Mouse " outfit and no, they were not, in fact far from it. In fact they regularly win awards.

At no time for the first two months of rehearsals did I actually think they would stick with me. I was always expecting the tap on the shoulder, almost hoping for it, but it never came. To make matters worse, the Director (Quasimodo, who managed to fall out with me and some of the other leading actors during rehearsals, which nearly lead to disaster for the play as there were threatened walkouts. Some people became very "Luvvie " and precious for a while) had decided we were not going to have a Prompt in HIS first Production as a Director– this is regarded as more professional if you can get away with it, but very scary. In the end, the cast- especially myself- asked for one and in spite of not being a very good listener he relented on this occasion. Suddenly, we were too close to opening night for me to run away, and it dawned on me that , for better or worse, I was going to have to go through with it. Then, before you could say "Break a leg ", there was Sir Wilfred Robarts, Counsel for the defence, in his QC robes and Wig staring back at me from the mirror in the (not my, the communal) dressing room, whilst inside the theatre the First Nighters were expectantly taking their seats. Me, I felt dizzy, thirsty and nauseous. Nerves just about under control....BREATHE properly!! I told myself.

" 10 minutes Sir Wilfred " whispered the ASM.

I"m not first on stage. ...What was my first line ...fuck, what was it ? Check the book. Music comes up ....we have lift off....Oh my God!

So, there I am on stage halfway through the first act and I am going quite well as it happens -I"ve even been able to tie my Bow-tie whilst spouting dialogue. A feat I was really proud of as it was a new skill learned during rehearsals which I didn"t think I would actually be able to pull off on the night. I was really cruising along , gaining confidence all the time. Suddenly, I "Dry", and there is silence from the Prompt who doesn"t seem to realise where we are or what"s going on. Perhaps she thought it was one of my "Dramatic Pauses". So I walk right across the "Stage in the Round " - with the Audience sitting on all sides of us - where she was sitting at the front in the DSR Audience with the Script open in front of her and just stared quizzically at her. She got the message, got the cue out, and I continued.

"Leonard Vole", the Accused, whom I was interrogating at the time, said afterwards he thought I had gone completely mad. All stage moves are carefully "Blocked " and rehearsed and I had just cruised past him to the other side of the stage , at a great rate of knots, entirely unscripted ! But amazingly hardly anyone else noticed– not even Quasimodo the Director, sitting in the Audience! "There you are

", he says afterwards. I told you you didn"t need a Prompt!!" Little did he know!

The next night I had had my usual pre night nerves which makes one very thirsty, but forgot to take the necessary drink of water– I spent the whole of the 1ˢᵗ act with a mouth like the bottom of a birdcage and could barely get my words out. An awful feeling. A bottle was always on hand after that, and "Props" put a glass on stage for me as a back-up. As you can see, things do go wrong on a fairly regular basis in amateur theatre, usually not the same things!But disasters do not just occur in Amateur theatre where you almost expect it.

I DO hope they weren"t disappointed in my performance. They didn"t seem to be and have given me serious roles since and, from my point of view, it realistically couldn"t have gone better. I don"t feel I let anyone down at any rate, and if survival without making too much of a fool of myself was my original aim, I perhaps did a little better than that. The Mrs says it was my best performance to date which may or may not be a compliment. The play itself DID win an award as it happens. This could be you if you just turn up like I did!!

Amusing stories and anecdotes abound in (Amateur and Professional) Theatre. There is a scene in the play we did after "Witness" , "Dear Octopus ", a well known play by Dodie Smith, Creator of 101 Dalmatians, where I play the Family Patriarch, in which there is a piano playing scene, and the actor in question couldn"t play. In this case a Dummy Keyboard was used on stage, and our Assistant Stage manager was to play a real keyboard offstage. I think on this one occasion she went for a Pee or something at the wrong moment, missed her cue, and the actor was left to play the piano on stage with no sound coming out. The audience realised something had gone wrong and thought this rather amusing, although the actor, and the director did not. I thought it was hilarious. The ASM herself was devastated at her mistake and took several hours(days?) to recover her poise! During the same play, on another night, I suddenly noticed a (Fire) poker beneath my feet and never remembered seeing it there before. Instinctively, I rather noisily kicked it out of the way, which was, of course, noticed by the audience. Unfortunately, unbeknown to me, that poker plays a leading role shortly after I exit that scene, and when the Nanny comes on she can"t find the poker!! The audience know exactly what"s happened to it, causing some considerable mirth!

Budding actors note: Always get onside with the Props and Stage Manager and ASMs–they can do for you with the greatest of ease just by hiding props you are about to need or failing to call you to a scene. You have been warned!!

After their plays" finish, amateur actors await the Critics reports with as much trepidation as a Pro. In our case on these productions NODA (Northern operatic and drama Assoc) and GMDF (Greater Manchester Drama Federation) were very kind and even complimentary. Awards were won for best supporting actor, direction and staging across these two productions. I"ve had some reasonable, even good "Crits " in my time and one or two not quite so good.

"Never act with children or animals " goes the saying. Well I beg to disagree. I"ve played with a few excellent kids-memorably in The Winslow Boy as the Boy"s father Arthur-in my time and I hope to do so again. In that particular play, my part calls for the father to be unwell, and to get gradually more ill as the play progresses. It wasn"t the kids fault that in the 3rd scene I completely forgot to take Arthur"s walking stick on stage, having used one in scenes 1 and 2. Did anyone notice though? You"ve got it– the director was the only person that did, and I got some "Stick" for my forgetfulness after the show finished that night. After that, I always left a spare hidden somewhere on stage! The next night I lost a line and couldn"t hear the prompt, which lead to a minor crisis for what seemed a liked ages before we got on track.

In another production, "When the lights go on Again " about the 2nd world war, I was asked to sing three solos. Three! I hadn"t sung solo since boy soprano in the church choir, had no singing CV really, and had no idea my singing voice was in any way acceptable, but the director was adamant. They say I sang " A nightingale sang in Berkeley square ", "Whose taking you home Tonight " and ""As Time goes by ", with "Some distinction for a non singer! " I"m still not sure if that was a compliment. In the last song I had to play dummy piano keyboard as per "Sam " in the film "Casablanca ". The critics subsequently put in their report that I "had accompanied myself on the piano ", to the amusement of myself and our director. They had clearly thought I was actually playing. What a laugh! Anyway it was great fun to do even if nerve wracking, particularly on opening night when 15 friends and acquaintances could be seen from the wings sitting in the front right by where my (dummy) microphone was located waiting to see what I was going to do this time! I nearly panicked but just managed to stay focused.

As a result of doing this particular musical it was discovered I can still hold a tune–after many years post church choir when I didn"t even imagine this was the case! Subsequently being "Headhunted " by the (world) famous Stockport Operatic Company to do "My Fair Lady " with them– a critical and popular success if ever there was one as it turned out and such great fun to be in -has confirmed this.

One common danger in amateur acting is the play going around in circles. This can happen when a Player has a set of similar lines to some earlier in the piece. Saying the similar line triggers off an automatic response from another actor who says the reply from the earlier scene and the play goes back about 20 minutes. Getting it all back on track is a nightmare.

Of course, the real curse of the not very handy amateur actor is being obliged to assist the set designers and constructors, particularly in the run up to the opening night when they are almost certainly behind schedule, and after the curtain goes down on the last night when you have to get out of the theatre at great speed to let something else go on. This work , however, should be avoided at all costs, particularly if you are, like me, not a fan of painting, decorating and DIY generally. For everyone else, its just fine. The following excuses should NOT be used as they have heard them all before:

Too tired
No good at DIY
Too old
Too young
Too ill
I am the Leading man/ lady and I"m too busy learning my lines etc
Its above me as I"m the Leading man/ woman and I"ve contributed enough in that capacity etc.

After our last play, I tried to lean on a flap as I was taking it down 12 " up a ladder with a drill in my hand. When it collapsed, I nearly went down. It could have been very nasty indeed. Not turning up is your best bet, although I have to say I wouldn"t dare not turn up! Anyway, the leading man or woman should never have "Airs and Graces" above their proper station, and if anything, make more of an effort to help in other ways!! All I can say is, I do my best to do so.

So what advice would I give a budding amateur dramatist?". My Top 10 tips:

1. Firstly, if you fancy having a go, do it! There are bound to be one or two "AMDRAM" societies near you all of whom will welcome new members of any age. Don"t be afraid of making a fool of yourself. You"ll be in good company. You will make new friends as a by product. I got into my current society because my wife found an advert for actors in our local paper. "Ring Jack on the following number.....etc".

2. Read the whole play several times and try to understand it and the allegories.

3. Try to BE your character.(Stanislavski "Method" acting theory) Think their thoughts, feel their feelings. Pace your performance and maintain momentum. Develop the character. Imagine how he/she would be. Use facial expression. The direction will help, but a lot of YOU will be required. Research the character–from the notes etc. and your own imagination. Be prepared to TRY things and the director can always change it.

4. Concentrate at all times when in rehearsal or on stage performing. LISTEN to what your fellow actors are saying. If someone, maybe you, maybe them, makes a mistake, you will be better positioned to deal with the mini crisis that may follow this. React to your fellow actors at all times as you would normally. Make eye contact as you would in real life.

5. Breathe through your nose and from your diaphragm.

6. Learn your lines as soon as possible. It takes the pressure off a little. This is more difficult for some than for others. There"s always a smartarse who turns up at the first rehearsal word perfect (and its NOT me, its John L at the Woodford Players

143

actually) and its not likely it will be you either, but do your best! It does make it easier to develop the character and learn the Blocking.

7. Take your own SPACE on stage.
8. Be physically FIT. Immediately pre-run and during the run you may have to play the part up to 7 or 8 nights on the trot, maybe twice in one day. This is tiring. Go to the gym.
9. Believe that you can do it and you will!
10. Enjoy it!

And why do I do it? Because there is great satisfaction and enjoyment in it when it goes well, and it puts me so far out of my comfort zone as its possible to be which I consider to be good for me in a perverse way! I have experienced times as an actor when I felt even a "Pro " could not have carried off a scene, or a moment in the play, better. Other times when, if the stage had opened up and let me drop through it, I would have been mightily relieved!

Footnote:

Jack, the societies Vice Chairman at the time, who was the first person at the society I had spoken to having put the advertisement in our local paper, made me feel really welcome and generally looked after me, giving me valuable and ongoing advice and his friendship. We also regularly went for drinks across the road in the Thieves Neck Pub. He liked a drink or two, did Jack. Jack, as it goes, played the Judge in "Witness " with, his usual aplomb. Two days later he hanged himself. Depression gains another victim. Jack"s due to serious money worries as he had been running about 30 Credit cards and owed money everywhere. He was a professional singer without a job. I regret his passing and I miss him even though I only knew him for a total of 6 months.Of course, much more than many others ever could, I understood how bad he must have felt to do that to himself.

CHAPTER TWELVE
ASPECTS OF WORK

One of the symptoms of an approaching nervous breakdown is the belief that one"s work is terribly important

Bertrand Russell

Real success is finding your lifework in the work that you love

David McCullough

Never continue in a job you don"t enjoy. If you"re happy in what you are doing you will like yourself, you"ll have inner peace. And if you have that, along with physical health, you will have had more success than you could ever have imagined.

Johnny Carson

All successful people men and women are big dreamers. They imagine what their future could be, ideal in every respect, and then they work every day toward their distant vision, that goal or purpose.

Brian Tracy

You must either modify your dreams or magnify your skills.

Jim Rohn

To my regret, in the end I didn"t really justify all the money my Dad spent on my Education from an academic achievement point of view, although from a life experience point of view it was a big winner. I am certain that my life would have been very different and probably a lot worse had I gone to the secondary modern rather than the privileged environment I did attend with its inherent opportunities! Anyway, a few years before he died, Dad was making a speech at a wedding or some event and, for whatever reason, made a point of saying how well I had done in my life. It was good to know he felt like that– as if I was being absolved from my crimes of leaving school early, not going on to University as he had hoped, and leaving job after job to try something else. The optimistically titled "Schools Career Advice Officer, one Mr Stephenson, who wasn"t actually a bad teacher had come up with a narrow range of choices:

"Army, Navy, Air force, Insurance, Banking, Accountancy, Law,"

End of! Is that all there is? Of course its not, but there were no other areas suggested for a departing private school boy who lacked imagination and didn"t think outside the circle.

I did eventually formulate have a plan of sorts – its just that it went wrong and was probably the wrong plan anyway. I had briefly wanted to jon the RAF as a pilot, or thought I did, so went for the 3 day Biggin Hill tests, but managed to fail as a potential pilot but I could have gone forward as a Navigator. Not interested thanks! Anyway, all this knocked me and my confidence back for a while. So I had to chose something else. Typically, I went from the sublime to the ridiculous. There followed a series of pointless office jobs which I just fell into without really giving it some serious thought. My first random choice was Life Assurance - what a dull idea, lacking imagination., particularly compared to flying. Talk about extremes. I joined the I.T Department as a computer operator -Yes that"s right. Metaphorically speaking, Computers were driven by " steam " in those days, the programme a printed circuit board that plugged into the side of this enormous machine that has far less computing power than the average mobile phone. One of the old stagers said the week I joined:

"The first 10 years here is the worst "

And continued

"But you will get used to it "

Well, I never did get used to it. The best thing about it was the girls, and the fact that you could smoke in the office, and go to the Pub next door for Beer and cheese sandwiches at lunchtime! However, in other respects, the tedium I suffered there for well over a year was much more than anyone should be expected to endure.It was not a bad job, but it didn"t suit me or my skills and personality at all. I just had to get out to search for something better. My Father was unimpressed I was leaving– his generation felt grateful to have jobs at all and most stuck with them. Baby Boomers wanted more out of life. Anyway, I left this first job a year later and joined a division of Uniroyal Tyre Company as Assistant to the Flooring Sales manager. Tredaire Carpet underlay- another uninspiring choice? Yes, that"s right..my search for the perfect job was not yet over! As it happens, it was better, but not by a whole lot. I had not thought about it properly and done what I should have done– go for something that may have been better, more enjoyable, more fulfilling and so on.

For me, right there, is Life"s biggest lesson for young people starting out- have a dream, live the dream.

Who says you won"t make it as an Actor, a Musician, a TV star, a Professional Sportsman? Someone"s got to do it, and why not you if you have the talent? In Life, I"ve found that you should "Ask for what you want ". Regrettably, I"ve not always done so, and I didn"t really have a "Dream " either. That was my misfortune. Ok, be a Lawyer, or an Accountant, and even join the now discredited Class as a Banker if you want to. Eventually I became a Banker, of sorts, when they got sensible salaries and bonus"s–just my luck to miss out on the big money - but they all want shooting after what they"ve put us through in recent times. Basically gambling on financial instruments most of them don"t understand.

Anyway, one thing"s for sure, if you don"t give whatever you fancy doing a try you will never know, and who wants to spend the rest of their life wondering? Life is too short to mess around just getting a job, even a reasonably well paid one. Pick something you may enjoy and change when you are young enough to do so.Then change again if necessary .The sooner the better. The older you get, the more difficult it will become to change over to a different career. One gets typecast very quickly. Johnny Carson was right- you are a long time out at work and they will be long days if you don"t enjoy what you do, believe me! So go for it!

With an early pay cheque I had bought a dog– "Captain", a cross bred Boxer– who,with typical canine lack of judgement , loved us all unconditionally from the moment he came into the house. Dad didn"t want to know initially, but by the end of his first weekend, Captain was his best friend. He cried relentlessly years later when Captain died, bizarrely of lung cancer as he was a non smoking Dog! But I digress.

Then , as it happens, having made a poor first choice, I DID set about trying to find a career that would get me up in the morning. I found it, quite by chance, and by being persistent in my search, and changed as often as I had to. I found it in something new , about which I had never heard. It was, in fact, a new (financial) product to these shores, and like many products before and since was imported from America. I got into it because, after the Bakery and the Store job, I needed a better job and FAST.. Finally I despatched myself on the train to the City of London seeking proper work and virtually took the first one I was offered. That turned out to be the bottom rung of a 40 year career in Invoice Factoring and Discounting! It could have been anything , but as a career its been more interesting than it sounds, albeit not a "Calling" as such! Ever since then I have had a severe case of the "Protestant work ethic"!!

I worked my way up over the years via Sales /Sales Management and Operations and eventually became a director of Alex Lawrie Factors Ltd, at that time about to become part of the Lloyds Banking Group. The "Hoover " equivalent of the Industry.

Then, just as I was doing really well there, after being a Director for about 3 years, and with the Northern Operation I had started a resounding success, yet another stunning opportunity came to me right out of the blue. Again I was onto it like a cobra striking!!

An American East coast Bank, First National Bank of Boston "FNBB", a couple of whose Senior Executives were vaguely known to me as they had shares in Alex Lawrie, were obliged by Lloyds Bank to sell their minority stake in us. It doesn"t matter why. Suddenly, they were unwillingly out of the burgeoning UK Factoring Market. It immediately occurred to me they might like to get back in– with me heading up a new venture in the UK and their Bank funding it. So I "flew a kite " and wrote a letter to the Senior Vice President that I knew , Clarke Miller, and he wrote back inviting me to go to Boston to sell the idea to their Board. Wow! I had, at that stage never visited the States, let alone flown Business Class. What an opportunity. I could hardly contain my excitement. They asked me to pen an outline Business plan, which I did. I still have it somewhere–it must be the most badly written business plan ever! Its also in longhand and had NO NUMBERS! I cringe to think of it– my second plan was a lot better, I can tell you.

I got a taxi from Boston Logan airport to the downtown business district, Federal Street. I searched in vain for a while for no: 100. I asked a passing Yank. Its up there he said, pointing upwards at a 50 story skyscraper. I had been looking for something a little more modest. I had no idea "FNBB " was the biggest bank in new England at that time! I stood in awe for a moment and then made my way in, heart pumping– don"t fuck this up Boy. From the 33rd floor where Clark Miller"s Secretary"s office was located, I surveyed the scene across the City from Faneuil Hall to the Cambridge river and Harvard university beyond. I had now DEFINITELY arrived. For three days I was grilled by everyone from the President downwards, and wined and dined quite royally, fish being the predominant fare–this, after all, was Boston, Mass!! Anthony"s Pier 4, Jimmys , Union Oyster House and the rest, serving tons of Lobsters and "Boston Scrod", and in between gallons of Chivas Regal.. fantastic. At the end of it they promised, in spite of the scruffiness of the Business plan, to put $ 750,000,in a London bank account and I could get started whenever. My new salary was mind–bogglingly large! They were to fund the loan book as it arose. I gave my notice to Alex Lawrie and left a month later.

Boston Financial was born in the most unlikely fashion but my goodness, what had I done!? I had left a company where I had been a star for 12 years to create something that I had no idea I was capable of creating. Now that"s going for it. That"s getting outside the "Comfort Zone". Not a moments hesitation or thought of failure and what might happen if I did fail. Everything was now on the line. But I didn"t fail and the rest, as they say, is history! Mind you it was very hard work indeed and I remember saying "never again" at one point. Four years later I sold the company to TSB Group on behalf of the Bank – at that time highly acquisitive- and I went with it . I personally made £125,000 in fees for running the transaction. This is how Boston went on to become Lloyds TSB Commercial Finance– a multi million pound company in its own right- making my reputation and putting me on the map. Within two years I had been earning twice as much as my previous MD!!

But after a while I started having other ideas– my itchy feet were at it again. I had forgotten how hard it was to create this thing and I was about to do something g rather "left field". Repeat the trick!

I have no regrets. I liked work. Like work even now. I did well at it, all in all, and rose to become Managing Director of three different companies each of which I founded from scratch, one as a subsidiary of the American Bank as above, one with Venture Capital, which I and the Venture Capitalists sold to N.M.Rothschild Bank, and after that another which we floated on the AIM Market, part of the London Stock Exchange. Proof, if you like, that University was not a pre-requisite for success in life and, in my view, still isn"t. Rather than attend a rubbish University course (although I accept that some careers need a degree) , why not just go out to work in your chosen area of work and work up? Remember you are earning money, learning a trade, and not stuck with huge loans at the end of the 3 university years! Simples!

Briefly, my guiding principles in life and business have developed as follows:

ANATOMY OF AN ENTEREPRENEUR.

Briefly, I feel the characteristics of a potentially successful Entrepreneur are approximately as follows:

Have some sort of dream or inspiration that they are prepared to follow.
Are prepared to get out of their "Comfort zone " and are ambitious–Very!

Risk takers. Unless you are prepared to take some risk, it is unlikely you will be a successful Entrepreneur!

People that never made mistakes, never made anything!

Someone who is a good leader and able to inspire and work through people.

Have an innate restlessness to succeed and challenge themselves.

Supreme optimists!!

> *"Success is the ability to go from one failure to the next without any loss of enthusiasm"*
>
> *Winston Churchill*

So what are the building blocks of a successful Business career? In my opinion:

FOLLOW YOUR DREAM. Dream of a job you would like to do or a business idea.

What is your vision.?

If it"s a business you want to found, RESEARCH the extent of demand for your product or service. Research what the competition is doing. Work out ways in which you can "Make a difference" in your chosen market place. Learn the value of good service and quality products in any market.

Remember the old adage - FAIL TO PREPARE, PREPARE TO FAIL!

BE or BECOME A SPECIALIST IN SOMETHING– understand your products and market or you will probably fail. Remember– you are up against competitors who DO understand it!

Write a BUSINESS PLAN with some milestones and some numbers attached. Set realistic financial and operational targets. Be able to defend how you constructed, for example, your sales targets.Work out how much money you need. Involve as many people as possible in the process to get both their inputs and their commitment to the Plan. Don"t exaggerate the potential of the business–it will come back to haunt you as Investors become disgruntled with progress.

MAKE A BUDGET and stick to it. Know your numbers and where they came from.

You need finance? Make the case for the business to sell to a Bank or a venture capitalist. Treat your bank or VC with respect.

CONSIDER THE RISK. Look at the downside as well as the upside. What could go wrong and if it does, what is the Plan B?

INVEST IN YOUR OWN BUSINESS–only then can you be seen to have true commitment. Why should the Bank and Investors put money in when you" ve not?

DON"T TAKE ON BIG OFFICES YOU CANT AFFORD. and take short leases where possible. You"ve no idea how big you are going to become and getting out of long leases can be expensive. Do you really need an office? Starting from home is often a good idea. Or a Business centre on a weekly basis for a while?

Give the IMPRESSION TO THE OUTSIDE WORLD that you are a bigger, more established business than you in fact are.(without lying!) e.g. make your home address seem like a business one.

YOU BE THE COMPLAINTS DEPT- this way you know what has to be improved. Give your mobile number to all the customers and all the suppliers for that matter.

MANAGE THE CASHFLOW and THE CREDIT RISKS. Businesses usually only goes bust when they run out of CASH. Don"t finance your customers- ensure you collect the money in efficiently and ruthlessly when you are let down. Don"t sell to bad credit risks. Check potential customer credit ratings before delivery. Spend sparingly only on essentials. Control the costs ruthlessly. Get as much credit from your suppliers as possible, and give as little credit as you can. Don"t overpay yourself/ves . How much money do you need to sustain the business? Arrange bank facilities in good time . In general terms ensure your overheads expenditure, wherever possible, are flexible so they can be reduced quickly in any downturn.

FIND A SUCCESSFUL ENTREPRENEUR and get him/her to Mentor you.

MAKE GOOD RELATIONSHIPS– with everyone, employees and customers/ suppliers included.

LEARN ABOUT SALES AND MARKETING– however good your product, it wont fly unless you can sell it. Where are your customers coming from.

HIRE GREAT PEOPLE– even if they are better than you. Look after them and treat them with respect. Go on a Man Management course and LISTEN to what"s being said. Employ as FEW people as possible and TRAIN them properly.

LEAD them, don"t bully them. Def:of a LEADER? Someone who has FOLLOWERS!! Look around and see if you have any.

DELEGATE where you can, which is more than you think you can.

RECOGNISE ACHIEVEMENT IN YOUR BUSINESS and reward it.

KEEP THE SCORE

Keep accurate and up to date accounts and Books and records monthly/ quarterly. Back of a matchbox is no good!

Know your numbers!

BE PREPARED TO "HIRE AND FIRE ".

If, even after giving them all the support, the employee doesn"t work out, GET RID. You cant afford passengers unless you"re an airline or a Bus company.

Keep checking what you are PAYING FOR GOODS AND SERVICES, ensuring you get the best deal. Build a good credit rating as soon as possible.

DON"T BE A "BUSY FOOL ". WORK BLOODY HARD BUT manage your time and really think about how you spend it. Delegation plays a role here. Delegate but don"t abdicate– follow up. WORK SMART.

Be prepared to work on your business 24 hours a day. REMEMBER, if it was easy, everyone would be doing it.

GOOD SERVICE is paramount- Under promise and over deliver your service, not the other way around. Its often your only point of difference. Put the customer first. Care for them, delight them, make them an advocate.

> *If you love what you are doing, and always put the customer first, success will be yours.*
>
> *- Ray Kroc*

GUARD YOUR REPUTATION and that of your business with your life!

BE PREPARED TO TAKE TOUGH DECISIONS e.g. laying off people early enough in a downturn rather than jeopardise the whole enterprise. Do everything that you can to keep your business afloat.

UNDERSTAND WHY YOUR CUSTOMERS ARE BUYING FROM YOU and investigate what else they might buy.

BE AN HONEST ENTREPRENEUR.

THINK LATERALLY–"OUTSIDE THE BOX".

REMEMBER–YOU ARE THE ONE TO IS GOING TO MAKE THIS HAPPEN, NO-ONE ELSE!!

And

DON"T BLAME OTHERS FOR YOUR FAILINGS

RETIREMENT

I must admit that, when I stopped full time work and "Retired " for a while, I became a bit confused and not a little bored. I felt rather useless without places to go, meetings, problems to solve, people to manage. Golf and Tennis, which I love, were, and still are, insufficient to keep me happy. They were always my reward for doing well in my job! I still do feel a bit useless if I don"t have anything to do, which happens only occasionally these days, but I must say I"m glad to not have to Manage people anymore. With the various employment laws, and other "Red Tape" these days, its becoming increasingly difficult. But without a proper job I felt diminished somehow. People who have been made redundant know how I felt. What I DID seemed to me to define what I AM and how others see me but, interestingly, this is not the case, I have learnt subsequently. I am seen as ME by many people, with or without my fancy previous job titles. They like me (or not as the case may be) for WHO I am not WHAT I am. This is good to know. Through working part time, I think I"ve now found a happy medium at my age. Many people look forward to retiring, then find its not all its cracked up to be, but then its often too late.

Statistically, many die within the first few years of retiring- you have been warned! One needs to keep one"s brain and body active! But I am now keeping myself busy part-time, and the cash flowing, through investments and Directorships. Just right.

One bit of good advice for anyone would be:

" Work hard and be as good as you can be " in your chosen profession. You can do no more!

Me retire? No, I plan to "Work "til I drop"!!

CHAPTER THIRTEEN
SKI THE DREAM

"It is not the mountain we conquer, but ourselves"
Sir Edmund Hillary, conqueror of Everest.

I love Skiing nowadays but this hasn"t always been the case. It Is one of the best ways of getting away from it all and relaxing you can have. Top of a mountain, fresh air, completely away in just a few hours from the worries and stress of working Life. Its fantastic. However, my early experiences of it were somewhat bruising, both to the " Ego " and for the body, and disappointing to say the least. Not at all what I had expected. I have now been skiing for some 30 years and am, I"m happy to say, a fairly competent participant. Getting to this position, I believe, has been one of my greatest life achievements, given what I went through to get where I am. It was a sport I had never got around to until well into my 30s as, in those days, injuries were commonplace and playing serious Rugby I couldn"t afford injuries. Simple as that. The reason for this is that the equipment was rather basic in those days of the 60s and early 70s. Leather Boots, wooden skis and poor non release bindings(you often see them hanging up in Mountain cafes) meant that Broken legs or torn ligaments were a regular occurrence.

Research tells me skiing on "wooden runners " has a history going back over 5 millennia, but for most of that time it was merely a means to get from A to B, not a sport as we know it today. The word "ski "goes back to the Old Norse word *skið* meaning "a stick of wood". Different types of skis have emerged at various regions at about the same time. One suggested original inventors of skis seem to be the people of the Sayan Mountains in Asia. Also skis may have been used in Europe during and after the ice age. The first type of skiing was cross country skiing, as a form of transportation, which then evolved into downhill recreational skiing. In later times, Pioneer Sondre Norheim, from Morgedal in Telemark, Norway has often been called the father of modern skiing for, around 1870, inventing the equipment and techniques that led to modern skiing as we see it today. Modern recreational skiing depends heavily on mechanized transport. Mountain resorts became commercially viable when city folk could reach them in winter by train beginning in 1868, Zermatt being the best example, and with the development of electrically-driven funiculars and aerial tramways beginning around 1880. The first known civilian ski race had already taken place in Tromso, Norway, in 1843, and then, in the late 19th century, Telemark skis revolutionized alpine skiing, being the first ski with an innovative narrow " waist" making it much easier for skiers to turn. So Skiing first developed as a recreational pastime in the early 19th century, which is much earlier than many people think. The first ski tour in the Alps took place in 1894 when the local Branger brothers teamed up with writer Sir Arthur Conan–Doyle --creator of Sherlock Holmes--for a traverse from Davos to Arosa. Conan-Doyle was living in the area as his wife was undertaking a cure for Tuberculosis. The first packaged ski holidays took place in 1903, to Adelboden, Switzerland, organised on a commercial basis by Sir Henry Lunn under the guise of the "Public Schools alpine sports club", which booked whole hotels for the first time. Winter holidays in Switzerland had become very popular with the British aristocracy since the first winter tourists to St Moritz in 1864. In March 1928, downhill and the modern slalom events were combined for the first time to form an open international alpine skiing competition, organised by Arnold Lunn and Hannes Scheinder in St. Anton, Austria. This event was to become the real starting point of international Alpine ski racing. But I digress.

I had left skiing until my serious rugby days were over, and went with some, by then, already proficient friends.

This was my first mistake- I should have gone with beginners like me. Needless to say, I had thought I would pick it up instantly and be very good. After all, had I not, in my youth, been a Water ski

Instructor!? Surely Snow Skiing was similar, requiring the same skill sets? How wrong can one be. My mate " Sooty", as it happens, was one of the experienced ones, and he took me to Sandown Dry slope in Surrey before we went to the mountains. It did not go especially well, I have to say. I felt unsafe and very awkward on skis, as if they were alien objects. Nevertheless, I completed a 6 lesson programme and got slightly better. Maybe 12 lessons might have been better? But Sooty was clear in his mind that, after this initial training on Dry slopes, once we got to the snow I was going to be able to join, not the Beginners, but the Intermediates!! I was flattered. Having no experience, I went along with this idea. This was my second mistake. Prior to the trip, I went and got the best gear money can buy. I really did look like a skier! Actually, I looked too good. On my first day I duly sign up for the " Inters ". Without further ado, we instantly head for a ski lift and go up, what seemed to me at the time, but in fact wasn"t, an enormously steep mountain. In fact, it was (approximately) a 400yd "Blue run" back to the village , Green being the easiest, Blue second easiest.(Red, "difficile ", and Black, "Tres difficile " are the next ones up). Not a problem if one is a genuine "Intermediate " but then I wasn"t, was I? I was now a Beginner at the top of a run that, basically, I couldn"t yet do.

I felt strongly that falling all the way to the bottom of the Run would be a possible outcome. I became rather nervous to say the least. Actually I was quietly shitting myself. There were 10 of us with a rather young and somewhat offhand French Instructor and we set off in a line down this, what seemed to me, frightening slope with plenty of snow on it. The others all turned out to be competent, and were doing what I now know to be "Stem Christies", what is the first step to Parallel skiing- the ultimate. I was doing my little "Snow ploughs" and not very competently either. Actually I was rubbish. I Fell over 5 times in the first 25 yards. I was making a real fool of myself. I readily admit I was scared stiff and covered in snow! I could hardly see any more as my goggles were full of the stuff, and not for the last time in my Skiing career! The Instructor was unimpressed with my efforts, although tolerated them for a (short) while before putting me out of my misery. I was clearly holding everyone up, not only whilst picking myself up, but also through the amount of time taken to put my skis back on– the bindings, it turned out,were too loose, and the skis kept coming off, even though my fastest speed could not have been much more than 3 mph. Eventually, he"d had enough of this, as had all the others in the group.

" You are too slow, and we must leave you" he informs me in unconvincing English.

Anyway, I got the message but this idea filled me with alarm. Would I get my money back was the furthest thought from my mind (I didn"t as it happens). The problem was, how was I going to make it back on my own?

To be fair, the village was only 375 yards away, if that. I could see it from where I was and I was hardly going to get lost! It was then that I made my 3rd mistake- I took my skis off and started to walk down. Any skier will tell you this is not a good idea, though most of them have never even tried it even if they ever saw a reason to! An hour later, I got to the bottom somehow. I was well knackered! I spent the next two hours by myself on a slope that was flattered to be called a slope, in that it was almost flat and, back in my comfort zone, I gradually regained my poise and, to a degree at least, my shattered confidence– a very important ingredient if you are going to ski well.

That afternoon, I joined the Beginners, which is clearly where I should have been in the first place! Thank you for nothing Sooty!

The next slope I went up was not as steep as the Blue, but still looked a bit to steep for my liking. Anyway, I got on with it and was now with my "Peer " Group as it were. And so my skiing career started at last, but skiing was supposed to be "Fun" and all the falling over etc was "part of the Fun". However, I"m sorry to admit I didn"t find this to be the case. All I wanted was to get competent quickly so I could ski with my Mates, from whom I felt very much "Semi Detached". Every evening I would return to the chalet absolutely worn out. I hardly had any energy for the Legendary Apres Ski one had heard so much about, but an hours nap before dinner certainly helped, and I would recommend the same routine to anyone. By the end of the week I had, it must be said, made some, albeit painfully slow and marginal, progress. But I left the Area– the Portes de Soleil - unconvinced I would be returning. Many don"t after their first trip.

As it happens, I"m glad to say, I did go back the following year, albeit against my better judgement. By the end of my second week-Val D"Isere that time - I had sort of cracked "Stems" and there was occasionally fleeting evidence of "Paralleling". Some of it was purely accidental as my skis came together against my will and I started plummeting down the slope until I fell over, or indeed threw myself over, since I hadn"t yet learned how to stop- a key ingredient in learning to Ski!

I was still in Ski school as I should have been, but I loved Apres ski, and in those days entered into it with a determination and dedication sorely lacking in my efforts to learn how to Ski properly. I was still falling over a very great deal but to be fair, that"s all part of the process of improving !

It was the Apres ski—and the companionship of my friends and new friends met out there- that kept bringing me back year after year in the early days. Eventually I developed the skill sets to go Off Piste.Once you are Off Piste, anything can happen of course . A case in point:

One bright morning some years ago, I was coming down off the Grandes Mottes glacier at Tignes with a few friends. We spotted a bit of Off Piste to our right— we could see tracks so assumed it was ok. We were happily skiing along, still not very far from the Piste, when, un-noticed by myself, I became separated from my chums just doing my own thing.I was skiing great and it was a lovely day. To my right I spotted a ridge clearly leading to a down gradient of some kind so I headed for it at great speed, intending to turn on it. Suddenly, about 20 yards from it, and for no particular reason that I can recall, I fell. I picked myself up and looked around— my mates were some way away waving frantically. I had just been about to ski over a 1000 foot precipice and my fall had saved me. I was only a few hundred yards from the Piste even then! Someone up there loves me !!(see " My Religion").

There"s an old true story of a skier freezing to death on a chair lift wearing the inappropriate gear- in his case a pair of jeans. Sometimes, albeit very rarely, the lift attendants miscount and leave a Skier on the lift all night by mistake, and that"s what happened in this case. Better clothing may well have saved him. Skiers can be fairly stupid and irresponsible at times.

People often stop school too early and end up with bad habits. I did just that. After several years, I got to a certain standard but I didn"t seem to be progressing, even though I was doing Black runs and getting around the Mountains, after a fashion, with my more experienced mates as I had craved. Eventually, I went for another couple of (Private) lessons–I hadn"t been to ski school for years. In one Hour this excellent Instructor, who I cannot thank enough, put me on a path that lead to immediate improvement and to serious improvement over the next few years. I had never been any good in deep snow, and " Steep and Deep" snow Off piste was virtually a no go area. He got me able to crack that, with a little help from the wonderful dry powder snow conditions to be found in certain parts of the USA. Utah is a great example. Snowbird / Alta, not far from Salt Lake City, home of the Mormons, the best example we have found. Their superb snow conditions makes it all seem like you"ve really cracked off piste powder– until one returns to Europe and reality that is! Still, it did get me going in deep snow, and I am better for it.

When you return to the Bar each night, do beware "Talking up" how good a skier you are. Better to err on the "Humble " side. Down play it is my advice. I suggest you watch a video of yourself before bragging, and even then DON"T BRAG!! My technique? Lacks grace and elegance I should say. More "Functional" I think. Lets just say nowadays I get around most places shall we, and I don"t often get left behind?!!

As soon as he was 7, I took my son (now a qualified ski instructor) skiing. Actually the whole family came.

However, the two ladies in our family, Mum and daughter, were not going to stay the trip, and after a couple of trips,my wife indicated her lack of interest in the sport. My daughter likewise though she has subsequently taken it up with some considerable enthusiasm and not inconsiderable achievement. Anyway, in those days of the 80s and early 90s, I usually took Adam to Steve"s chalet in St Gervais, near Megeve, along with a load of my school / rugby mates and their kids. It was ideal. On other occasions, we often got in Steve"s People carrier and would ski the awesome "Grand Montets " at Argentiere, (and the adjacent more forgiving Red and Blue runs below., near Chamonix). Take two cable cars, and you arrive at the top of the most wonderful series of black runs, which fall nearly 4000 metres to the valley below. Take 2 cable cars to the top of the Aguille de Midi in nearby Chamonix, and ski the Vallee Blanche with a guide. Access is by an ice bridge and one is roped up. The last lap down is done by Mountain Train. You wont regret it!

Actually, I remember now. I used to blame the skis for my performance, so I kept changing them and buying new ones at great expense (second hand skis are more difficult to sell than second hand Durex.).As I say, I now always hire the best so I cant do that anymore!!

Just ski AND BLAME YOURSELF WHEN IT GOES WRONG and go and get some more lessons!

CHAPTER FOURTEEN
FROM "BORN AGAIN " CHRISTIANITY
TO ATHEISM- A JOURNEY

"When I do good, I feel good; when I do bad, I feel bad.

That"s my religion."

Abraham Lincoln

"True religion is real living; living with all ones soul, all ones goodness and righteousness."

Albert Einstein

"At least two thirds of our miseries spring from Human stupidity, human malice and those great motivators and justifiers of malice and stupidity, idealism and dogmatism and proselytizing zeal on behalf of religious or political Idols."

Aldous Huxley

The worst thing you can say about God is that he"s an underachiever".

So said Woody Allen, my all time favourite comedian but, on reflection, I think perhaps he was wrong. I think the worse thing you can say is that God doesn"t exist. That"s what I feel. I say:

"God is no more than a superstition. A myth"

This is now my strong belief. And as for "organised "religion in general….I have a real problem with that!

My generation have, of course, as a group, deserted the churches and religion itself in our droves since the 50s and 60s. If we can believe a recent survey by the "Humanist Society ", an Atheist group, only one third of UK citizens now believe in a God. It is said that, in the 70s, some 5.4m people attended the Christian church on a regular basis. That number has now shrunk, staggeringly, to 3m whilst the population has risen startlingly. Also, half of the 16-30 age group have no Christian background, nor do they foresee a Christian future, whatsoever. That said, many people do still harbour an uncertain belief in a God of some sort, so they play it safe by subscribing to "Pascal"s Wager" or "Gambit " that suggests in effect:

"It is just as well to believe in God, as if God does exist one might gain eternal life, and if he does not, then nothing is lost "

In my experience, this is effectively the position many, many people take, but I will not as I see the position as too much of a compromise . Having been brought up a strict Christian by my Mother, I ultimately determined to make my own mind up, and not settle for the "Wager " position. I looked at the FACTS and studied my true feelings. Over time, I came to various conclusions that moved me in a different direction. One that took me ultimately from "Born Again" Christian to Atheism. As a child I was given religion by my mother who was keen on it– devout even. I became a church goer, a bible reader, a Crusader, and a member of the church choir, at least until I was 16 or so. I was confirmed, then later became a "Born again " Christian. A simple ceremony performed by my Crusader Group leader, committing my life to God in a prayer. Just like that. Actually, it all seemed rather unconvincing at the time and my faith, such as it was, didn"t last long after that. I decided not to confuse rousing hymn singing and ceremonies, companionship and somewhere to go for a social, and nice biblical morality tales, with the likely existence, or otherwise, of a God. Tellingly , I lost count of the number of clergymen who, rather disingenuously I feel, were able to tell me exactly what "God" was thinking, or what his opinion was on any number of subjects at any moment in time. Of this ability I became, in the end, very suspicious indeed.

I had read the Bible cover to cover - how many people can say that–so I do feel I am qualified to comment on the Bible from knowledge.I came to the conclusion, in the end, that its just a "hotch potch" of stories and writings, tales and myths, some interesting and informative, some less so, all written by mere mortal men, full of glaring contradictions. A reliable historical record it is not! A source of knowledge for scientists it is not! It is also not, in my opinion, the "Word of God". Why? Well, first of all its written by Man of course. Gospels chosen at random and just put into one book along with all the other stuff. Some gospel writers left out altogether. Of course we know that clergy of different persuasions interpreting the bible themes in different ways has also caused many rifts and persecution of one sort or another.To be fair, I actually rather like large parts of the bible. Some good stories and morality tales.The Good Samaritan and all that, Noah"s Ark, The Ten Commandments and so on.

Ironically, I have always WANTED to believe in a God–it would be really good in many ways. Unhappily, I now regard God, presented as a kind of imaginary "Celestial Dictatorship", as a rather unlikely phenomenon, and live my life on the assumption he does not exist. This is a position with which I am now very comfortable. One question, to which I"ve never had a satisfactory answer and about which religious people freak out when I ask them is:

"If God created the world, who created God?"

It seems to me a reasonable question to ask. He couldn"t have created himself, surely? It"s a bit like thinking about the boundaries of "Space". How can "Space" have an end? How can you create "Space"? It"s too mind boggling. For thousands of years there was strong belief that we, the human race, are somehow special in a universe at the centre of which is the Earth. Well, we"re not really special are we? We are animals- albeit highly sophisticated ones - like any other in a small place in the apparently never ending galaxies and universes that surround us.

FAITH VERSUS SCIENCE

In 1633, Galileo pointed his telescope at the heavens and what he saw challenged the received wisdom of the Catholic church in particular. Galileo observed that in our Universe,   many planets were going around many suns and other planets, and by definition that NOT everything orbited the earth. This directly contradicted religious teachings, so in retaliation the church found him guilty of hereticism. Pope Urban VIII was prepared to see his erstwhile friend literally hauled over the coals by the "Inquisition" in order to prove that this new science nonsense was a fad that would not last.

In the beginning the explanation was God.Then, in the age of science, Charles Darwin changed all that, speculating that it all began in a "Little warm Pond". The origin of life was, up to a point, explained, and it was not by a "God " in seven days about 45,000 years ago,which is still believed by a fanatic minority.

Since the beginning of historical times there has existed a deep schism between religion and science. Some high profile scientists such as Capernicus were indeed murdered by the Catholic church for revealing inconvenient scientific truths. For 150 years since Darwin, religion and science have been locked in argument   about   Creationism" ("Intelligent design") versus Evolution. Many Believers treat the teachings in scriptures as LITERALLY true– the "Word of God ". Religious groups around the world have fought to ban the spread of the "Theory of Evolution" and in Tennessee classrooms, by way of example, it was banned for many years, as a result of which for decades many American children grew up knowing nothing of Darwin. However, as it happens, the founding fathers of America, feeling Religion and politics don"t mix, had actually banned in The Constitution religious teaching in their public schools but it went on anyway. Later, in 2005, an American court upheld a plea from a group of parents that the teaching of "Intelligent Design " was religious teaching dressed up in other clothes. Unhappily, the Church"s assumed monopoly on "Truth " has always threatened enlightenment, and continues to promote myth as fact and even tries to put the onus on science to prove there isn"t a God! A popular objection to us Atheists" arguments against Theism is to suggest that one"s favourite God cannot be disproved! Indeed, that science itself is unable to prove that God does not exist. In fact, in a very real sense, it is possible to say that, scientifically, God does not exist, just as science is able to discount the existence of a myriad of other alleged beings. My belief is in Darwinism, which is proven scientifically but even so, often denied by the Religious . How odd to believe in things that can"t be proven and not believe in things that can! Blind faith continues -American and other Evangelists, for example, will just NOT have it that the earth was created billions of years ago. The Bible says it was only a few thousand years ago by "God", and that"s it for them. End of. However, research informs me that the presence of "Man" in England, as an example, goes right back at least a staggering 500,000 years to "Boxgrove Man", discovered a few years ago in West Sussex. He–or rather bits of him- can be seen in the Natural History museum. This rather "pisses on the chips " of the extreme "Creationists" and it is increasingly difficult, even for Theists, to hang onto the myth that says we are all descended from is Adam and Eve! The best scientific models currently suggest Homo Sapiens were a population of about 10,000 breeding individuals living in Africa about 150,000 years ago. It seems that, if Adam and Eve aren"t literal, we might as well just throw the bible away!

While not strictly a competing code of belief, science has clearly attracted the wrath of misguided Popes.

I certainly agree with the Founding fathers that religious belief and politics don"t mix well. Be very afraid of the political Leader who proclaims "God tells me what to do when I pray ". Or "I am guided by God " and any variation on the theme. To me religion seems to stand for blind belief, dogma, bigotry, exploitation, and the preservation of vested interest. That explains George W Bush, Tony Blair and Gordon Brown then, all of whom are self confessedly religious and, perhaps even talked to imaginary beings asking for their advice and guidance . Scary! Did God tell Blair and Bush to go to war against Saddam Hussein? I suppose it would be nice and comforting to think there is someone up there who listens to us billions of people individually at whatever time of day or night when in prayer, and that there is a "Life after death " in a beautiful "Heaven " but does it really seem likely ? Actually, I have no issue with "Faith"–it must be a great comfort to many–but even if I did believe in a "God", I would not wish to be part of organised religion of any denomination. For me it was, as much as anything else, the hypocrisy of so many religious people that drove me away from my faith, and the petty intellectual arguments that Church Leaders waste their time on drive me nuts. For example, one such argument concerns the Catholic religion"s theory of "Transubstantiation"- that the bread and wine ARE the blood and Body of Christ not just representative of it. This seems to me to be , well, just nonsense.Yet they argued for it, and persecuted and tortured people about it for years.

And then we have some religion"s ongoing problem with ordaining women. More nonsense, and very Sexist, but this time its leading to schism, and many, many disaffected anti - women ordination Anglican clergy are now deserting to the Church of Rome , thereby reversing 500 years of History since Henry V111 caused the split to allow his divorce with Catherine of Aragon to proceed. This is really damaging the Church Of England, but they only have themselves to blame. Could God, even if he really did exist, really be a "Sexist "? Why not ordain women bishops ?

As with some of the American Evangelists these days, it is interesting to note how quickly the "Soul" was saved as soon as the money jingled in the Church"s moneybox! The idea that " Gods Pardon" or "Penance " could be bought even if there is a God is patently ludicrous, but persists to this day. A deeply religious man himself, many of Luther"s Theses deal with his anger over this issue. The Catholic church has amassed disproportionate riches in exactly this way, and in exactly the same way as the modern day " Evangelists". The manifest hypocrisies of Popes, and Bishops and other clergy for that matter, over the ages are right there in the history books should you care to read them.

THE CATHOLICS

The highly questionable conduct of the Catholic Church over many centuries is worth dwelling on for a while, starting perhaps with the notorious Borgias in the 1400 and 1500s. A strange and rather frightening family, the Borgias. Eleven cardinals of the Holy Roman Catholic Church. Three popes. A queen of England. A saint. A family with long tentacles, beginning in the fourteenth century in Spain, and reaching through the history of fifteenth and sixteenth century Italy, Spain, and France. Greed, murder, incest. And clearly -- strangely - piety. Such is the legacy of the Borgia family that established itself in one of Italy"s most glorious periods, and that, in many ways, dominated the Renaissance with power and intrigue for fifty years. In a number of ways, it was a heritage whose influence on Church and State was felt for two hundred years. Of this notorious family, four members in particular are remembered as remarkable examples of greed and evil. Two were popes: Calixtus III (Alonso Borgia) and Alexander VI (Rodrigo Borgia). Another, Cesare Borgia, was, for a time, a cardinal, elevated to that position by his acknowledged father, Alexander VI, and later, after leaving holy orders, a murderous and ruthless duke. The fourth member has become a metaphor for feminine evil: Lucrezia Borgia, sister of Cesare.

For some reason the world"s 1.3bn Catholics still doff their caps to the capricious, largely Italian bureaucracy at the Vatican, even with its shady past, which they believe is the gateway to heaven. Popes identify themselves as descendents of Peter the apostle and Catholicism identifies itself as the church Christ intended to build. We are lead to believe that each new incumbent is effectively hand picked by God . But, through the centuries, Popes haven"t always been " whiter than white" as one would imagine with such a divine creator and I have already mentioned the Borgias.

The most controversial Pope of modern times was Pius XII, who took over in 1939 and was labelled "Hitler"s Pope" by those who accused him of turning a blind eye to reports of the Holocaust. He did so, they claim, in the firm belief that it was better for the church to drink with a dictator who killed six million Jews than it was to condemn him and risk seeing him replaced by "Godless" communists. However, the offences of some of the Popes pales next to the rousing recruitment appeals for Crusaders that Pope Urban II made at the end of the 11th century. Those who helped him forcibly eject Muslims from Jerusalem and much of the Middle East were promised eternal salvation as their reward by Urban himself. So when the First Crusade reached Jerusalem in 1099, the entire population - Muslim and Jewish - was massacred, an act for which the papacy only apologized in the late 1990s. Benedict has stolen a march on his predecessors in this regard by issuing his mea culpa in just 24 hours. If it took the Popes a millennium to say sorry to Muslims for the Crusades, and it needed almost two before they asked forgiveness of the Jews.

Far from being a glowing example to the world of Christian values, the papacy spent much of its first thousand years being passed from one disreputable scion of a Roman family to another. Stephen V1 (896-7) decided to exhume the corpse of his predecessor but one, Formosus (891), so that it could stand trial. Dressed in the Papal Vestments, it unsurprisingly offered no adequate defense and was condemned to be mutilated and thrown into the Tiber. And in what was a low point for the sexual morals of the papacy, in 954 the 18-year-old John X11, the son of a previous pope, took office and turned the Lateran - the papal palace before the Vatican - into a brothel, and was ultimately murdered a decade later by an outraged Cuckold who found him "in flagrante" with his wife.

And then, like a breath of fresh air, Martin Luther appeared at the dawn of the 16th century during the reign of King Henry VII and pinned his 95 theses to a church door in Wittenburg, Germany in 1517, which lead to the subsequent rise of the Protestant religion all over Europe. One of the most powerful weapons used by the Protestant reformers of the 16th century against the Catholic church was to detail quite how unsavory were some of the men who had managed to get their hands on the keys of The Vatican.

Even with this disastrous past , the Catholic Church claims a monopoly on the deepest truths of humanity and the universe, yet couldn"t even properly deal with its own most recent, and perhaps biggest, crisis- the Priest paedophile scandals across the world- slipping into some sort of paralysis of inaction. The first high profile prosecution for child abuse was Irish priest Father Brendan Smyth in 1994, but a subsequent enquiry concluded in 1999 that the last FOUR archbishops of Dublin had known about the crimes of their priests for the previous 20 years and had concealed them!! Literally Thousands of children between 1914 and 2000 had been affected according to the Ryan Report and some offenders were actually promoted to get them out of the front line.

All we can hear, even now, is the sound of these things being swept under carpets by the various authorities including the police. Everyone, it seems, was afraid of taking on the catholic church.

The Church has clearly been a rather unnatural home for a remarkable number of Paedophiles as we know from the many Priests around the world caught at it in the name of God. Some of them, thankfully, have now been "Outed ", but I"ll have a wager not all. Hypocrisy at its most stark by those in positions of most trust.

I cannot for the life of me understand why anyone would wish to join such a dreadful Institution. Henry V111, in the 16th Century, did us English a very great favour by, for the wrong reasons, taking us out and forming the Church of England.

It seems the Vatican is ripe for reform but I can"t see that happening, can you? They too are losing members in droves.

Meanwhile, a declining Church of England has spent far too much energy recently debating the supposed unsuitability of women for high office , rather than get on with the business of rebuilding their disastrously falling numbers. They also need reform or, at the very least, an injection of realism.

A MORAL CODE

In my opinion, we don"t actually NEED Religion to have a moral code, albeit that"s where I got mine alongside my parents strictures. Religion and its Theists believe they have a monopoly on morality but it"s a common misconception that morality requires religious belief. Modern moral thought is often said to have been rather indebted to Mill—an Atheist— and Kant, whose views are based on "Practical reason" rather than religion. Aristotle,a philosopher, was Pagan, and his life predated religion by hundreds of years. It seems ethics is not a branch of theology, but of philosophy, since the time of Socrates BC.

My biggest issue , to which I have already alluded, is with organised Religion itself and with its manifest hypocrisies and disastrous conflicts, internal and external, over centuries. Even if I found out tomorrow there really IS a God, I would still have a problem with organised religious practise in most of its forms. And I"m not picking on any one religion. Religion itself seems to have caused more problems than it has solved. As far as I can see, the carnage has been created within and by most religions. It was only 3 centuries ago that people were being burnt at the stake in England and elsewhere for believing in the wrong kind of religion.They believed in God, but not the official interpretation at the time. So called "Heretics " were being dealt with "left, right and centre". And not believing in ANY God was just unacceptable- I would have been burned just for penning this. In the name of Religion we have seen often innocent Witches persecuted between 1400 and 1750 in particular, Crusades, Serb/ Croat and Muslim massacres, Jews persecuted for being "Christ killers". I believe strongly that people must be allowed to practise a faith or NOT practise a faith without fear of persecution in either case. During the "Reformation", Henry VIII was hanging, drawing and quartering, or burning at the stake Heretics and the like as he crushed the rebellious against that reform and brought the country into line, all in the name of religion. It was a tyrannical time. As we speak, shiny haired Television Evangelists fleece naïve people out of Millions of pounds many can ill afford trying to buy Gods forgiveness, and disport their ill-gotten wealth in most unseemly ways. What do the victims think they are buying? A place in the myth that is "Heaven"? More fool them.

Religious belief and its conflicts has caused all sorts of problems. In India, they partitioned the country. Pakistan for the Muslims and India for the Hindus. Many died. Religion is demonstrably divisive and make no mistake,it can KILL.

"My God is better than your God ".

A possibly non-existent "God ", through the scriptures , allegedly "Promised " the Jews Palestine, which lead to the displacing of many, many thousands of Palestinians creating havoc in the region since 1945 or so.

All over the World religious faiths are in conflict with each other and the divisiveness religion creates is manifest: Sunni Muslim versus Shiite Muslim all over the Middle east, Catholic versus Protestant as with the Northern Ireland troubles and so on.

ISLAM

Nowadays, fanatic jihadist Muslims blow up themselves and innocent people in the name of "Allah " - 9/11, 7/7, and so on - for a promise of "Eternal Salvation", "Virgins in paradise for all eternity.. etc". .

What happened to " Thou shalt not kill?"

But where did they get their motivation from to go down this road?

What does the Qur"an ("Koran ") say on these matters? Surely not to arbitrarily kill fellow humans, including innocent women and children!

Well, unbelievably, it does seem to say just that, as the following extracts demonstrate, and frighteningly , these are highlighted for emphasis in the website I looked at and it seems to be page after page of (to paraphrase):

"If you don"t follow me you will burn in Hell" and "Fight, Fight, Fight ......"

Woeful punishment seems to await Non- Believers ("Kafirs ") , but for the Believers– 1000 million of them to date - there"s:

"Virgins as fair as coral and rubies.." and loads of other benefits including eternal life...

Well I never! It"s all in there.

And it goes on:

" Islam- the sublime,single and transcendant truth..."

"Fight in the cause of Allah (the one God) those who fight you"

"Fighting is prescribed for you"

"Take not into intimacy those outside your ranks or they will corrupt you "

"For the unbelievers are to you open enemies. Soon we will cast terror into the hearts of unbelievers "

"To him who fighteth in the cause of Allah so we will give him great reward"

"The unbelievers shall be gathered together to hell"

"Fight and slay the Pagans wherever ye might find them "
"We drowned those who denied our revelations "

...and I could go on. 400 pages dominated by this sort of rubbish. I could hardly believe my eyes.

Not very positive messages to say the least, but it is now quite clear where the Extremists get their validations.

What seemed to be lacking was any logic, evidence or reasoning to support this nonsense.

Just " Follow me or you will die ".

There is an awful lot of rubbish in the Old Testament, but the Qur"an takes the biscuit. Read it and be very afraid.

So who wrote the Qur"an?

It is not known for sure but it is widely believed by Muslims it is the word direct from God given to the founder of the Prophet Muhammad which the Prophet is supposed to have written down. "Celestial dictation " if you like. These were the "Revelations " he experienced one day when was meditating, searching for the truth. Apparently, he awoke shaking and a voice came to him with a divine message from Allah. It was the Angel Gabriel! (him again)

This is all a big claim but there is no equivocation amongst Muslims. No " ifs or buts or maybes"! The word of God (Allah) received through the Prophet Muhammad. And what a mean God he does seem. But the problem is Muhammad was probably illiterate, so what credence can we give any of this ! Probably not much!

Muhammad, the founder of the Islamic religion, was born in Mecca (Arabia) 1400 years ago, 600 years after Jesus was crucified. He lived the first 4 years of his life as a Bedouin Tribesman but his mother and father died when he was very young and so he was brought up by relatives, having a hard early life by definition.

Before Muhammad, Arab tribesmen believed in many Gods. The Prophet was told to establish a proper Muslim community, which he did, in Medina, but in the early days he and his followers were persecuted for preaching monotheism. Then later, through Africa,

Persia (Iran) and Asia, the Muslim armies brought the news that God was all powerful. "The one true God ". Interestingly, Muhammad"s God is apparently the same God as that of Moses and Jesus.

For the sake of balance and all that said, Muhammad is alleged to have preached more positively, but contradictorily:

"All innocent life is sacred "
"To save one life is to save the whole world "
"Destruction of infrastructure forbidden"
"There is to be no compulsion to follow Islam"
"Do not drink wine "
"Do not fornicate "
"No falsehoods

WHICH RELIGION?

So, if you believe in a "God " and want a "Faith", which religion to follow? Seems to me this becomes, for the most part, a matter of into what environment you were born and brought up.

If you were born in the American Mid West, and you think Christianity is true, or if you were born in Afghanistan and think that Islam– the opposite- is true, then, either way, are you not a victim of indoctrination, as it is clear the most important thing is where you were born and by whom you were indoctrinated? No single religion appears to have any greater claim to being more credible than any other. Why Christianity and not Judaism? Why Islam and not Hinduism? Why monotheism and not polytheism? Every position has had its defenders. They can"t all be right because they contradict, but they can all be wrong. In one Religious book I read many years ago, its opening line was "There must be a God, or why are we here". This is errant nonsense. Why does there HAVE to be a God? Can there not be another answer? Of course there can!

Mind you, I personally don"t have a problem with people having a "Faith" if they wish- that is their right and it must be a great comforter to many people, but it can only be a FAITH.

But how do we make our lives meaningful without a "God " and perhaps a belief in a life after death?

My response is merely just look and wonder at nature itself–it"s so beautiful and fits together so well, how can we imagine it was created in the same way as a car? Darwinism and natural selection-"Survival of the Fittest" (which does, I admit, sound a bit selfish,) provides the answer.

It seems to me that what matters is the kind of society that our collective belief systems create. Do "Religious " beings live "Better " lives than non believers? A fascinating study in the "Journal of religion and society "(VOL 7 2005) and reported in the Times Sept 27 2005, found:

"In general, higher rates of belief in and worship of a Creator correlates with higher rates of Homicide, juvenile and early adult immorality, STD Infection rates, teen pregnancy, abortion rates in the prosperous democracies, and early adult mortality ".

I wonder how it is that theist belief creates, or at least doesn"t eliminate,such failings in man?

Have you ever seen the "God Europe " Channel on TV? Do! Have you ever heard such rubbish? Turn it on one night and I guarantee that, even if you do harbour some belief in a God, these guys will put you right off!!

Religion has been used to control the Masses, often, in my opinion, through the deployment of FEAR. Still is. Scaring us about "Hell and Damnation " if we don"t conform. Going way back to Emperor Theodosius, who saw religion as a way of uniting his fragmenting Empire circa AD 378 and, before him, Emperor Constantine patronising a struggling Christian Church. Without these two, it is claimed, Christianity would never have gained the hold it has today. In my view, often as not, it is being afraid of not believing - FEAR of what may happen to them after life. A Fear that has been instilled by religious teachings for centuries. "If you don"t believe in GOD you will go to HELL" is, in my view, as much a superstition as the belief in God itself. The threat is "You will be consigned to Eternal Damnation". For me, I couldn"t believe in such a man, or whatever HE or SHE is. He seems to lack humanity. Just read Genesis for further proof of that. All that said, its fair to say that I don"t actually KNOW there isn"t a God, but I don"t need to know this and just make the assumption there isn"t. And what about the animal kingdom- and at the end of the day we are all animals, albeit humans are usually more sophisticated animals. Do they go to " Hell" automatically, because they don"t even know about " God " and certainly don"t go to Church?! Asking for "Forgiveness for our sins" becomes very hypocritical after a while. Ask God for his forgiveness, then go right out and do it again. That always struck me as rather generous of "God " as described to me.

> *Different men seek after happiness in different ways and by different means, and so make for themselves different modes of life and forms of government.*
>
> *Aristotle*

> *Dignity consists not in possessing honors, but in the consciousness that we deserve them.*
>
> *Aristotle*

As for HOW to live a "good life " - albeit at best "goodish"? Well perhaps a selection of some of the 10 Commandments, or "Decalogue" , is a good start point for a moral code. I like a few of them. The rest are merely religious laws which don"t apply to me. Here"s the relevant ones:

> *Honour your father and mother ....*
> *You shall not Murder*
> *You shall not commit adultery*
> *You shall not steal*
> *You shall not bear false witness against your neighbour*
> *You shall not covet ...anything that is your neighbours*
> *Love thy neighbour*
> *Etc etc....*

Well, five out of sevens not bad! Coupled with avoiding the " Seven deadly Sins " should cover most of the bases? I do feel strongly that Religion however , with exceptions, has too often not turned out to be a force for good but has tended to poison almost everything it touches.

Well known Atheist Professor Richard Dawkins tells us:

"The usefulness of a belief does not prove its truth."

In any case, many societies have thrived without these beliefs, while crime has thrived in theistic societies believing in "heaven and hell". You cannot define or imagine a thing (in this case a "God") into existence. Professor Dawkins also tells us :

"The burden of proof lies first and foremost with those making the claim — the theistic, religious believers who say their "God" exists. Non-believers don"t need reasons not to believe. "

To believe in any God for me would now be a real stretch, and I"m no longer susceptible to being frightened into believing, that"s for sure!. Having failed to find any real evidence that God exists, after many years of looking, I am now an Evolutionist. Atheism has been seen as a dirty word, so I don"t use it lightly to describe my belief systems. I have really thought about it. To have proclaimed myself "Agnostic" would, I feel have been copping out. Science has of course, provided many of the answers from Big Bang -13.7bn years ago- onwards, so, under those circumstances, is there room for a God anymore? Do I feel I need to carry on my search for a God? No! It seems to me that the beauty of the universe is enough.

To be born, to wonder, to enjoy life, to procreate and die is the accepted order of things. It is far from bleak. To be without religion is not to accept emptiness as the alternative. One answer is, of course, that to live as good a life as possible is enough and this is how one finds a kind of "Heaven on Earth " and inner peace? It also seems to me (and EM Forster) that:

"Friendship, warmth and honesty between people matters so much more than any "cause" or "system" of belief. For me, this is a practical, as well as romantic, ideal."

Albert Einstein wrote:

"I don"t try to imagine a personal God; it suffices to stand in awe at the structure of the World, insofar as it allows our inadequate senses to appreciate it"

I like all that, and it encapsulates my beliefs too. Its the sort of thing that we can hang our hats on to give life meaning in the absence of religious belief ourselves and for me its not a compromise. Religion is, in my view, just "mumbo jumbo " shite, and I say this whilst conceding there are precious pockets of good that flow from it.

However, the perpetuation of myths, the sheer hypocrisy, intolerance and sheer stupidity of religion eventually put me off it completely.

I agree with the late Christopher Hitchens that, at the end of the day, Religion is the source of ALL tyranny.

CONCLUSION

Space is very large indeed and , for the moment, just "Is ". To demonstrate the size of the known universe , lets take a Light year which is 10 million, million Kilometers per year. We are now able to see light that has travelled from the very edge of the known universe and has take 13 Billion Light years to get here!! Wow!

So just WHY are we here, on this place called earth, right in the middle of the "Milky Way " Galaxy, all alone so far as we can tell amongst literally billions of galaxies? Of course the fact that we don"t know why doesn"t prove the existence of a God either.

At the end of the day, however, I am still left with a feeling of: "What"s it all about "?

It is, for now, a mystery, but in my view, not one that can be explained away by inventing something called "God ".

It is also a mystery that I can live with .

CHAPTER FIFTEEN
HELLO SAILER

Twenty years from now you will be more disappointed by the things that you didn"t do than by the ones you did do.

So throw off the Bowlines. Sail away from the safe Harbour. Catch the Trade winds in your sails. Explore. Dream. Discover.

Mark Twain

Everything can be found at sea, according to the spirit of your quest

Joseph Conrad

The two happiest days of your life are the day you buy a Boat, and the day you sell it.

(Anon)

Today is the second happiest day of my life. I"m selling my boat, "Ocean Wolf " named after my rugby club. The happiest was the day I bought it, but the happiness didn"t last very long. To be honest., Mark Twain"s above quote has been more use to me as a metaphor for life than something to be taken literally as pertaining to sailing.

The first time I went sailing was 30 years ago with Sooty and Ginger. It could quite easily have been my last. It was 1979, and a lady who was to change the face of Politics had just come to power- Margaret Thatcher of course. "The Iron Lady". She became a bit of a heroine of mine.

Ginger owned an all wooden "Morgan Giles ", a 27 footer that had seen better days. It looked a bit like a "Folk Boat ". "Fallander" was very scruffy and also, as it turned out, ill-equipped to make the journey we were about to undertake. As were the crew and its skipper. We were all, as it turned out, making the trip for the first time. Um!

We slipped our mooring, and sailed quietly out of Salcombe harbour one friday night "As the Sun sank slowly in the west" to cross the English channel, headed for the Channel Islands– Guernsey first stop! As became clear some hours later , none of us knew what the fuck we were doing as I will demonstrate! It was a rather warm and fairly typical mid -summer night with a certain amount of breeze to fill our sails, and we were, no doubt about it, very excited. There was only a slight "Swell", it was cloudy and no visible moon to speak of. It was my first trip in a sailing yacht and I was going with experienced sailors. Or at least, that"s the impression I had got in the pub before we left, where several pints were sunk.(Drunk in charge of a sailing vessel? You bet!)

We went out into the open sea and all seemed to be going well. I didn"t know what I was doing, so I listened carefully for any instructions that may come my way.

"In the kingdom of the blind, the one eyed man is King",

and I concede Ginger, and Sooty for that matter, knew more than me, but not much. As it happens, not many meaningful instructions came my way, with the exception of the occasional "Pull this, caste off that, stow the fenders " and so on. For the time being at least, the two of them seemed to have it all under control. This was great– I had always wanted to try sailing. I was relaxed and chuffed..as it happens, not for very long. "Control" was not what they had at all, as it subsequently became very clear!

Two hours later we entered the first of the two main shipping channels which one always has to cross when heading for France or The Channel Islands. In the English Channel there is a "Separation Zone" whereby ships heading east stick to one channel, and ships heading west stick to another, with a "No go zone" in the middle– and one has to negotiate both, sort of at right angles. Night was falling fast. The

Channel carries an enormous amount of commercial shipping, and they come down over the horizon at you at a great rate of knots, literally. It is actually the busiest shipping lane in the whole world and we were about to negotiate it AT NIGHT and for the first time!

Additionally I was with two "Sailors "– I use the term loosely- whose combined total knowledge about sailing was, unbeknown to me, the "Square Root of Fuck all ".

For example, according to the "Book", a competent Skipper, in our case Ginger as it was his boat, must have a number of Skills:

He must:

Be able to handle the boat in ALL conditions (Er, not as it turned out, no!)

Be familiar with the boat and its equipment (we didn"t have much equipment as such)

Be trained and ready to deal with emergencies. (Whoops!)

Understand the regulations (another whoops!)

Be able to forecast weather (Sian Lloyd off the TV he was not– on the way back we ran into a bit of a un-forecasted storm– see later in this chapter)

Provide the Crew with training (In my case I was provided with approximately zero training including NO safety briefing- essential - or any briefing about how things worked)

Must be a good Leader (oh dear!)

Delegate (no chance)

Supervise (If you don"t delegate there"s nothing to supervise– you get to do all the work)

Additionally, the boat must be well maintained (Oh dear again!)

I now know that crossing these shipping lanes is a hazardous exercise not to be treated lightly, but I got the impression at the time were about to enter a "Cake Walk". It wasn"t long before all we could make out were the twinkling lights of ships large and larger going about their business. We couldn"t see the actual ships at that point, but it turned out they were huge tankers, freighters, coasters and the like going up and down at similar speed. It was quite pretty, actually. You could occasionally make out their shapes when they got close to you but that was about it. Some of the lights seemed to come quite close to us but Ginger was unfazed:

"Motor gives way to sail " he announced confidently.

Much later it dawned on us that in these shipping lanes it doesn"t, or at least it doesn"t do so very often, in spite of the fact that it is legally obliged so to do. Sailors could perhaps reasonably expect that any oncoming vessel would have a man on the bow peering out into the dark, would see a little light, send a message to the bridge, and the ship would turn away. The problem is, with lower manpower aboard and more electronic systems, they are far less likely to have such a lookout, and yachts do not make good pictures on radar. Apart from anything else, and even if you are spotted, the big ships can take some sea miles to "Answer to their Helms".In other words, they can"t change course quick enough to go around you even if they were inclined to. Also, they have places to go, cargoes to deliver on tight schedules. They can"t be messing about for a bunch of wankers on a small sailing yacht. They"ve seen it all before,and, no question about it, run right over a few without even noticing (surely not on purpose??) As it happens, sailing boats do quite often get mown down in the shipping lanes by far larger vessels, to the extreme detriment of the boat and its crew. Any sailing boat"s demise is rarely reported or noted in the press, so we were naively unaware of the dangers before us! Sometimes, boats just disappear, and nobody knows what happened to them. Clearly, then, yacht skippers must make the assumption they will not be seen, even in daylight, and act accordingly. We were making no such assumptions. Missing these big ships is a matter of judgement - does one try to go in front or must one wait and go behind them when they are gone? It can be a fine line and a lot depends on making good choices.

To assist, one usually has the help of a very useful piece of equipment called a "Hand held " compass. If regular checks on this reveal the same bearing—the course - of the ship in question, then you are on an eventual collision course and must take evasive action, as it is unlikely HE will. We actually did have one of these on our boat, but it was never used for this particular purpose. We ploughed on, completely unaware of the dangers we were facing, in a south westerly breeze force circa 3 - 4, and under a full sail, we were "Close Reaching". Quite a comfortable "Point of sailing". We were quite enjoying ourselves actually ("In the

Minds of Innocents....") and there were surprise compensations- for example at one stage, and for an hour or more, we were surrounded and followed by a school of porpoises. Magical! Seagulls were constant companions, looking for scraps of food thrown overboard. I often, on future voyages, had the same experiences, sometimes with dolphins. They are so friendly– almost seeming to be trying to communicate with us. Luckily, there was no sign of any albatrosses. For now anyway! Ginge and Sooty (so nick named because he once threw a bag of Soot at someone)– whose sailing skills(oxymoron in this context) in those days, albeit obviously streets ahead of mine, were rather limited to say the least.They were , however, giving the impression of great expertise in the art. But my doubts were growing as we managed to miss a couple of big ships by what appeared to be a few feet, on one occasion actually having to turn tail as one monster bore down on us, but carried on believing they were all trying to miss us regardless.However, it seemed both of my companions were much more concerned about the navigational aspects of our voyage, rather than the safety aspects. For example, at NO STAGE during the voyage, or the week ahead, did ANY of us go anywhere near a safety harness (which clips one to the boat preventing man overboard) or a lifejacket!!!! We were, however, happily walking all around the deck, AT NIGHT, going about our chores. If anyone had fallen overboard we would NEVER have found them in the dark and anyway we hadn"t practised the drill for retrieving a man overboard as you"re supposed to do before leaving port.

Anyway, we had to hit a tiny island some 80 nautical miles away with the aid of nothing more, it seemed, than an "AA map and a piece of string " (q. Max Wall circa 1965). We certainly had no GPS device ("Global Positioning System ") in those days– they were yet to be invented. Basic navigation was all we had, very similar to Captain Cook"s I would imagine, some 250 years before, less one sextant. On the plus side, we did have radio beacon signals to tune into which, if you can get three , give you some idea of your location. Unhappily, these are desperately difficult to pick up and interpret(trying and failing to work this funny contraption made me feel dizzy, then sick)

Believe it or not someone HAD actually remembered to bring charts of the areas we were planning to sail on which we (they) could set and plot a Course and practise " Dead Reckoning " etc by calculating average speed , direction of travel etc– difficult and inaccurate enough by day, but at night....! Whether we had an up to date copy- or indeed ANY copy- of the relevant "Channel Island Pilot " book is another matter. I cannot for the moment recall seeing one. They even kidded themselves at various points during the voyage that they knew where we were, although I dare say we were heading in the right general direction as, to be fair, we did seem to manage, from time to time, to gat an approximate "Fix " on our position, but were never really sure how accurate these were.

Crossing the Channel, as we have seen, there are all sorts to contend with, including of course the tidal streams which, coming into you from the side , send you one way for 6 hours and push you the opposite way for another 6 hours and so on. They can be very strong, particularly during what are called the "Spring Tides" or "Springs ", and in light wind conditions, can often be going faster than the boat, as we found out when we hit the notorious "Alderney(Tidal) Race " at the wrong time when visiting Alderney Island from Jersey a few days later. In these circumstances, you end up going backwards. This is a very depressing experience as the entire objective is to get to the nearest onshore pub as quickly as possible! The main thing that affects the tides and their intensity is the orbit of the moon, unlikely as that may seem. Anyway, what you have to do is to adjust your main course on a regular basis to account for this. You steer into the tide to keep,as far as you can, your intended bearing. If you don"t, you might get swept to America. At best, this adjustment is an approximation. They had both passed their "Day skipper " Theory exams which deals with some of these issues and I was initially impressed. I shouldn"t have been. Theory is one thing, putting it to practical use is quite another. "Yacht Masters" they were NOT! What they didn"t know exceeded what they did know by a factor of about 10:1

The first thing that we didn"t realise was that a couple of our navigation lights weren"t working, so even if ships wanted to change course to avoid us, they couldn"t see us, or they were going to find it difficult to work out in what direction we were headed.! We had no distress flares either. Disaster was just around the corner. For the time being, however, we were having the time of our lives, although blissfully unaware of the dangers before us.

Then I started to feel sick again. Seasickness was not something I had ever experienced but here, outside the sight of land, I felt like SHIT. For those of you who have never suffered, it is the most AWFUL feeling in the world.

You want to die. "Skipper " had nothing in the medicine chest to help me (actually he didn"t have a medicine chest OR First aid kit AT ALL!) This feeling went on for several hours with me fighting the inevitable, and I was duly sick as a dog at about 2 am in the morning, and continued to feel sick for the rest of the night. I retired to my bunk. The others were not impressed. It was alright for them– they didn"t ever seemed to get seasick, which always put me at a disadvantage. However, my "Sea Legs" did arrive by the time we docked and happily I was never sick again during the two weeks away, nor for the rest of the summer, so it could have been worse. Some people suffer all the time and still want to sail.I wouldn"t!

After about 12 hours of this pitifully slow progress– I was still in my bunk- someone shouted "Land ahoy ". Sooty had spotted a lighthouse beam, and, checking its signal on the chart, (x number of flashes short / long in Y seconds enabling us to locate it on our map) we realised we were approaching the lighthouse near the Little Russell on the southeast tip of Guernsey. Well, I couldn"t for the life of me work out how this was possible, and for a while doubted the situation. I needn"t have. After 14 hours of (VERY) basic navigation, indecision, cock-ups, confusion, equipment failure, missing large ships by the length of a " Midges Dick ", sickness etc, we HAD actually arrived at the place for which we had been aiming!! No doubt remained. A miracle had occurred (see the chapter on religion) 2 hours later we were moored up in the Marina at St Peter Port (Guernsey"s main Port) tired but happy as my seasickness had disappeared into the night from whence it came.

St Peter Port, as it happens, is a great little place with its (Fish) restaurants, Quaint Pubs, Bars, and even a half decent nightclub with a pretty half–naked girl dancing in a cage suspended from the ceiling. I wonder if she"s still doing it 30 years later? I love St Peters Port and have returned a few times since on boats that were, shall we say, rather better organised than "Fallander". Things were definitely looking up. From there we visited Jersey– where we had to stay for a few days as the rudder broke on the way over - Sark, Alderney and Herm. Charming places, all of them. When we were in Jersey, we met an old school colleague and Actor, who was in a play there at the big Theatre in St Helier, which was being Produced by Cameron Mackintosh in his early days. This was 1979 remember. We saw the play, and went out afterwards with some of the cast. One or two of the Girls were quite fit- one was the very well known and gorgeous actress Cheryl Hall who was married at that time to the actor Robert Lindsay who it turned out was in the midst of a steamy affair with his now wife Diane Weston- so we took them all sailing the next day. We had a good laugh.

The days passed pleasantly exploring the islands on and off the boat and soon enough it was time to head back to Salcombe. Too soon for me– I was by now having a great time. In Port, where I talk a "good game ", I am one of the most accomplished sailors you have ever met ! In fact, I was dreading the return voyage and a sense of impending doom came over me. We couldn"t leave at the appointed hour as there was a storm over the channel.

Not a good start. Leaving a day late, Gingers weather forecast indicated all was now calm, so we headed off down the Channel towards the Little Russell once again. I now know this area to be notorious for its unsettled and choppy seas-it is where various conflicting tides and winds meet. A bit like Portland Bill. It suffers more than some parts of the Channel in "Wind over tide " conditions which result, often as not, in very choppy seas (as we have discussed, the Channel islands have some fearsome Tides) and we were heading for trouble. For the moment however all seemed fine. Then suddenly all hell broke loose and we were in it!! No warning whatsoever. Suddenly the wind came up, the seas were a morass of foam and we were experiencing the biggest waves I had seen since our Surfing trip to Newquay. Bigger. Huge and I"m not kidding. The Boat was being pitched this way and that and disturbingly we had a full set of sail up, large genoa (foresail) and mainsail fully set. We had to reduce, and quick!

"Don"t panic, Captain Mainwaring!"

We leaped into action. Sooty disappeared! Skip reefed the "Main ", not without problems, but he did it.(Still no sign of a safety harness) He then headed for the foredeck to get the large "Genoa " Sail exchanged for the more appropriate " Storm Jib ". I was on the Helm and Sooty, I could now see, was shitting himself in the main cabin, probably because it was me on the helm!! He may have been praying, I suppose? No matter what the Skip did, however, he couldn"t seem to get the Genny off. The shackle was rusted! Surprise surprise! (see "maintenance" passim) Get the WD 40 out! BUT, you"ve guessed it, they couldn"t find any! Over my right shoulder comes another yacht within shouting distance to ask if we were alright (I said we were even though we weren"t,) and to point out that "Some of your Nav lights are out ".Tell me something I don"t know Pal! Skip was supposed to sort those before we left Guernsey! I, however,have for the first time on a yacht, got my wits about me,. Partly because I"m not feeling sick, I had remembered reading a book about sailing the Atlantic by celebrated yachtswoman Claire Francis, and she had emphasised the extreme importance of sailing at an angle into really big waves. So I did, and it worked because we are still here to tell the tale, and not capsized and at the bottom of the English Channel, somewhere near Guernsey. However, we weren"t out of the woods, as we hadn"t had time to plot a course.So suddenly were we into this nightmare. I was guessing where we were going and, unbelievably, it was night again. For all I knew, we could have been headed for the rocks off Guernsey, placed there for the purpose of sinking us. We certainly had no time to consult a chart, put it that way! This all carried on for a couple of hours at least, maybe a lot longer - we lost track of time— but Skip did eventually sort the storm jib, and had managed to reef the mainsail to its smallest pocket handkerchief size. He was also able to give me a bearing and we were heading home! As for me, well I began to feel almost like a sailor!!

After that trip for years, on and off, I would sail with Sooty who eventually bought his own yacht and did become proper "Yachtmaster". Some years later he met my work P.A. Christine, fell in love and I lost my P.A. and my place in his crew! They now happily spend much of their time sailing the south coast, Brittany and The Med. What a good life!

Sailing has been fun over the years - I"ve been up and down the channel many times to picturesque places like Poole, Weymouth, Cowes, Isle of Wight, Dartmouth, Salcombe, Falmouth, Brittany and the Channel Islands several times, Ireland three times, and the notorious bay of Biscay as far down as La Rochelle. Its been by no means all bad news.

BUT-here"s my advice:

If it " Floats , Flys, or Fucks, RENT IT".

So goes the famous old saying. Well I didn"t remember that when the time came.

" Do you want to buy and share a boat with me?" says my mate Shuff", an Ocean Yachtmaster and Round the World sailor off the Chay Blyth "Round the wrong way " circumnavigation, somewhat disarmingly. After almost no (rational) thought I said:

"Yes, why not, should be fun".

Apart from fleetingly– for example the occasional great trip and the search for just the right boat which took us all over the country- it wasn"t really much "Fun ", but it was very expensive,and often dispiriting for various reasons. The trips to Ireland were "Fun", and some of the trips around the Bay were "Fun", but the Holyhead Marina fees and the repairs , and the cost of the de-fouling and the improvements, and the purchase of the dingy and outboard and the rest of the gear you need were not" Fun". Nor was the notoriously unsettled weather in North Wales "fun"- in fact it was often rubbish, especially, it seemed to me, on those rare occasions I had booked a weekend or even a few days into a busy diary to visit my expensive yacht. In truth, I didn"t have the time to use mine nearly enough to justify owning it.

I had always said I would NEVER buy a Boat, especially in North Wales, so why did I? I still can"t work it out, but let it be a lesson to all my readers. Think twice and think again, and even then DON"T BUY a yacht. Don"t do it!. EVER! Sail with friends in their yachts or rent one with them when you need to.

Today is the second best day of my life, because as I write this, a sale is agreed and just going through. I can now go sailing in the Med where the Weather is warm , on rented yachts, with some other friends. Yippee!

But some years later and now armed with my new "Skippers Certificate ", Croatia, and the Antigua Race week, here I come!!

CHAPTER SIXTEEN
RECONCILIATION

Eventually, back in 1985, me and the Missus did get back together but she was very unsure about it, and it was a very loose arrangement for some time. I was still working in London and just appearing at weekends, but I was well paid and for one thing that did facilitate was paying the school fees. Eventually, I gave up a good job to come back up north permanently, and we were able to have a proper family life with the kids. The family years passed amazingly quickly. Looking back, it"s a bit of a blur but I must say I loved being a taxi service and getting involved in the games and activities with which my kids got involved . I miss all that I don"t mind telling you. Overall, they were a joy to bring up.

Then, all of a sudden it seemed, they were gone. There were just the two of us again– we had only spent 9 months or so alone in 20 years. When the children were around she never seemed to notice me as I came and went. Looking around the house she came across me one day and, deprived of children to organise for the first time in years, she started organising me! For the first time she wanted to know where I was going and when I was coming back!

We slept in the same bed together, me and the wife, for about twenty years- except during the separation, of course. Then one day we stopped–just like that! I snore and she"d always put up with it. Often she would take refuge in the spare room. One day, finally fed up with my snoring and always being the one to go to the spare room, she kicked ME out of the Marital Bed. "Laugh and the World laughs with you. Snore and you sleep alone".

As it happens, sleeping apart had several advantages and I found that I liked it. I know she felt the same.

I liked the freedom to read– to put the light off when I wanted,to listen to the radio, the TV, and pick the station I wanted. To not be woken up. No more causing each other sleep deprivation, accidentally waking each other up all the time! And the amount of room in the bed. Wonderful! But surely to want to sleep alone is a sign of a broken marriage. Well maybe it often is, but apparently, many years ago, the upper classes rarely slept together. It was regarded as a sign of wealth if you didn"t. It was considered poor form to sleep together all the time, and, if you think about it, it doesn"t really make logistical sense. Cramped together in too little space– much too little. No need for it at all. Of course, as a young married couple, we wouldn"t have dreamed of sleeping alone but it made sense the older we got and the idea is becoming both fashionable and even aspirational again.

How about that, we helped set a modern trend! I understand the arrangement is on the up on both sides of the Atlantic. It"s a very personal thing of course but its certainly very practical even though people may well be embarrassed about admitting they sleep alone. We never were as it happens, and were relaxed enough about it to openly discuss it. Statistically at least, sleeping apart is said to lead to MORE harmonious marriage in many cases, but perhaps not in ours! Separate bank accounts– we had those too- has the same effect apparently. Strange but true.

Relations with Mrs S were friendly most of the time but we eventually drifted further and further apart and a minor argument could erupt at any time into short-lived battles of will that you will find in most marriages. From my point of view, I feel she always had to be right and I always wrong. From hers? I guess I didn"t listen and I didn"t tidy up or do much around the house. I probably didn"t actually and have never been trained for the job but I am very clear about what I DID Do. I could say that, if she wanted my opinion, she"d give it to me, but I"d better not. I never wanted to be an absent father where someone else becomes "Dad" to your flesh and blood. It makes me shudder to contemplate it actually. Remember Ginger"s Kids were taken "Down Under " by his ex–wife"s new man? Monogamy is hard, and we are clearly not all programmed for it, but multiple marriage doesn"t seem to be any answer at all. Eventually, an infidelity by me did for our marriage, but in truth it was dead already. How sad after so long.

Remember though- marriage teaches you loyalty, forbearance,self restraint, patience and many other qualities you wouldn"t need if you were single!

CHAPTER SEVENTEEN.
"LOOSE ENDS"

"Life is either a daring adventure, or it is nothing"
Helen Keller"

"He is a man of many talents, all of them minor"
Leslie Halliwell, Film Historian
(who clearly knew me well!)

"Carpe Dium"

("Seize The Day ")

You will never find time for anything. If you want the time,
you must make it.

Charles Buxton

Any man can win when things go his way, it"s the man
who overcomes adversity that is the true champion.

Jock Ewing

So there you have it– a shatteringly worthless and somewhat vulgar life captured in shatteringly worthless and vulgar prose. A literary genius I am, demonstrably, not. Nevertheless I am proud of my efforts. Its honest, perhaps too honest, but is that a bad thing? I hope its not too upsetting for loved ones because it is delivered with love and affection and I feel it does have its moments of gravitas. I have enjoyed the writing of it over the last three years or so, much more than I would have thought. The process of writing the book has been a little like rummaging around in an old trunk for items long lost. My own story has, surprisingly, come back to me quite easily, in a fully rounded fashion, as I have been penning it. I didn"t think it would when I started. All in all, it has been a cathartic exercise. As an inevitable by-product to my story, I hope I have enlightened as to the prevailing "Zeitgeist " of the 50s, 60s, 70s and beyond and informed over the various subjects and events that have touched me and about which I have written.

The post war period has been an unprecedented period of wealth and excess, invention and achievement and world peace promoted by nuclear weapons. I hope I have brought some good memories back for fellow Baby Boomers and enlightened the younger generation just a little as to what life was like for us all those years ago.

Us Baby Boomers have lead a life of unprecedented freedom, safety and affluence. Conceived following the rubble of wartime and the deaths of so many sons and fathers, we have enjoyed very different times. We are truly "The Lucky Generation. So many life changing inventions have happened in my lifetime. So many of us have central heating and damp proof courses—do NOT under- estimate the benefit of these- shorter working hours, money, television, computers, WWWeb Access, cars, houses, mobile telephones, IPods, better healthcare, more and often foreign holidays and travel, better life expectancy, consumer comforts, a far wider choice of leisure activities, and so on and so on. We have seen man land on the Moon and experienced no world wars in our lifetimes. We have seen the creation of the Welfare state, now out of control, and we have spent and spent and left our children to pick up the tab of the debts and the pensions we have awarded ourselves because successive governments have failed to plan properly and borrowed and borrowed. It is a sobering thought that the Baby Boomers will probably be the last generation to be able retire at 65.

The following, freely available on the Internet, sums up some of the changes during our time:

"First, we survived being born to mothers who smoked and/or drank while they carried us and lived in houses made of asbestos.

They didn"t get tested for diabetes or cervical cancer.

Our baby cots were covered with bright coloured lead-based paints.

We had no childproof lids on medicine bottles, doors or cabinets and when we rode our bikes, we had no helmets, not to mention the risks we took hitchhiking.

As children, we would ride in cars with no seat belts or air bags.

Take away food was limited to fish and chips- no pizza shops, McDonald"s, KFC, etc.

We ate cakes that mother made, white bread and real butter and drank soft drinks with sugar in it, but we weren"t overweight because......

WE WERE ALWAYS OUTSIDE PLAYING!!

If there was no school, we would leave home in the morning and play all day, as long as we were back when the streetlights came on. Soccer on the "green" down my road a favourite.

No one was able to reach us all day and we were O.K.

We did not have Play stations, Nintendo Wii, X-boxes, no video games at all, no video/dvd films,

no mobile phones, no personal computers, no Internet or Internet chat rooms.........WE HAD FRIENDS and we went outside and found them!

We fell out of trees , got cut, broke bones and teeth and there were no lawsuits from these accidents. My mate fell out of a tree and broke his wrist right in front of me trying to collect conkers.

We were given air guns and catapults for our 10th birthdays.

We rode bikes or walked to a friend"s house and knocked on the door or rang the bell, or just yelled for them!

Mum didn"t have to go to work to help dad make ends meet! Her job was to look after us.

RUGBY and CRICKET had tryouts and not everyone made the team. Those who didn"t had to learn to deal with disappointment. Imagine that!! Getting into the team was based on <u>MERIT</u> .

Our teachers used to hit us with canes and gym shoes, or threw board dusters and chalk at us, and bully"s always ruled the playground at school.

We had freedom, failure, success and responsibility, and we learned

HOW TO DEAL WITH IT ALL! "

Someone once suggested Life, in essence, is about LUCK as much as anything else:

"All of the good luck and all of the bad luck and the balance between the two that one gets in one"s own life ."

Well,I certainly believe that, up to a point, one makes ones own luck through ones own efforts, but also some people are more unlucky than others in the end. Many Baby Boomers have been VERY lucky indeed, including me.

> *Do not go where the path may lead, go instead where there is no path and leave a trail.*
>
> *Ralph Waldo Emerson*

Looking back over my Life, I feel I"ve achieved much and done some very good things and some very stupid things.I have certainly cocked up here and there where, with the benefit of hindsight, I would have acted differently. I have some regrets but relatively few. It is a bit of a tale of "extremes " of both sadness and varying degrees of happiness, but mostly the latter laced with some contentment and frustration. As I pen this, I find myself happier and more content than I have been for many a year, but history tells us this could all change in a moment of unforeseen crisis at some point in the future.

I like to be "busy". "Busy " is good isn"t it? Busy means we"re hard at it achieving our "goals" without excessive time to stop and think and look around. I have to say every time I"ve stopped to think, I decided I wanted to be busy. I know what it"s like not to be "busy " and I didn"t like it one little bit. We complain of another year gone–"where did that one go "? And it is best at that point to reflect and see if we actually achieved anything that year and make adjustments for the year to come. Put your time where your priorities are. We only have limited time on this earth and its best to use it well I guess. Still we all have to make a living, even if its doing something we don"t like!

However, disturbingly, I"ve rarely managed to experience a sense of pleasure when projects were over.Once something had been achieved, I never felt that I had reached journeys end but merely empty.

The "Wellingtonian melancholy of the Battle won ".

Success did not taste as it had promised and this I have always found unsettling. What new worlds were there left for me to conquer, I wondered? Thus we can deduce the real fun was in the doing of the project, so I always had to find another project. I still feel like this. I am truly a helpless victim of the "Protestant work Ethic ". Without a project I feel utterly, utterly useless, so I mean to have at least one on the go at all times until the day I die. I think this must be the lot of the "Driven" man, but I am still unsure as to whether I have achieved my full potential in life so I must keep going. Nevertheless, keeping active is a good thing in my opinion. I have been all over North America, Africa and Europe in particular on business and its been fun. Like all Baby Boomers I"ve been very lucky in that I missed the two World Wars by a whisker. We should all feel very grateful for that. I don"t handle rejection well- a Psychologist would probably say it was because an elder girl cousin rejected a Christmas present I carefully prepared for her when I was 8 or so! Perhaps there are other things that happened in my childhood that also are the root cause of some of the more negative aspects of my life that some expensive visits to a "Shrink" would unearth, but I see no point now in deploying the finance to check this out. My overwhelming desire to please and be liked in life has often of course,when I"ve been caught displaying these traits, had just the opposite effect. That said, we don"t really know what people think about us unless they happen to tell us, so assume nothing!! That said , however, I do feel I have enough friends, acquaintances and relatives to be going on with, and a great bunch they are. I mean to ensure I taste all the available delights of life before I go, but the list is shrinking as I"ve been lucky and done so much.

After my depression experience described in chapter 1, I did spend some time in the famous Priory Hospital in Roehampton long before it was fashionable, and I was completely out of it for days on end. I was drugged up to the eyeballs, and slept a lot. Initially days of sleep, then more pills and sleep, chats with the Psychiatrist, and then group sessions with the other Inmates.

That said, I was clearly not as depressed as the completely "Bonkers " ex -Public schoolboy from a well heeled family who was committed to the Priory because he kept chucking himself off buildings and somehow surviving. He was a nice lad much younger than me but very unhappy. Some months after he was let out for the umpteenth time, I heard he eventually did succeed in killing himself, and in that particular way. How sad. Now he was a REAL depressive of the manic kind. Luckily, I have only suffered after a couple of seriously negative events that happened to me in the past, and not on a regular basis.

Whilst inside, I was given doses of the notorious ECT. "Electro Convulsive Therapy". Putting pulses of electric shocks through ones head at regular intervals for about ½ hour whilst under general anaesthetic. An electric stimulus is briefly applied to the head to induce a seizure. This is thought to treat the illness although the precise mechanism by which it works is still unknown. ECT has been used for approximately half a century but there is still a great deal of controversy surrounding its use. Nevertheless, it seemed to work quite well on me as I always felt better after these sessions, and it probably did contribute in some mysterious way to my rehabilitation. It also apparently helps Carrie Fisher-Princess Leia of Star wars - on a regular basis! During the admission process I had been so unwell, I convinced myself I would never come out again, let alone survive to regain my job, which I did . Time has been a great healer—all this happened 25 years ago. There were compensations once I was in recovery mode. It was quite a social scene in The Priory. I won"t mention the Celebs who were there in my time to protect their privacy, but I had a blast with them once I started to feel better! Great companionship with people most of whom were not "Mad "as such. A Sort of club really. (Not at all like the infamous Epsom hospital Longrove, which I briefly passed through on my way to The Priory, which was ghastly and frightening). In fact the inmates in the Priory seemed surprisingly normal. It seemed totally safe and cocooned in there. A real "Comfort zone". But I"ve never wanted to stay in those for too long. Now I"ve been there, I definitely do NOT want another bout of clinical depression-it"s the worst thing there is, in my experience, and most people just don"t understand it which is unhelpful. If there is anything worse I, for one, do not want to get it. Ok, motor neurone disease is worse. You may be surprised to learn that I consider getting well again after my depression one of my greatest achievements. Back in the swing with exercise, doing normal things, going to the pub with friends, all with the support of my family and the Shippards who played a key role as the story started to develop. Playing tennis, golf, going to the gym and even taking up rugby again all helped, as did getting back to a normal working life. For me, the real healer was the safety and seclusion of the establishment and time to get well in a comfortable and supportive environment. The illness just seemed to run its course. In the end one just has to "Pick up ones bed and walk ...."

I was away from work several weeks in the end, and am ever grateful to my American bosses who kept my job open so I was able to pursue my project to its eventual, highly successful conclusion. I left this company, that I founded from an idea 27 years ago, four years later , to get back home to Manchester,when it was making a tidy £1million net profit a year - it now makes over £100m as a subsidiary of Lloyds TSB!

After exploring my life through writing this book, I still cannot see why I should have got such a debilitating depression when there are millions of people worse off than me who haven"t experienced such a terrible illness. I wouldn"t wish the experience on my worst enemy. It may, I suppose, have been in conjunction with some sort of "Mid life crisis" which just made things seem even blacker than they were in reality, although I cannot say that marriage break-up, or, say, losing one"s job, is anything other than a miserable experience for many. Everyone, of course, has anxieties, worries, fears, problems (at least I think they do) but these are absolutely amplified and become obsessional as depression takes a hold. Vincent van Gogh, Sylvia Plath, Ernest Hemingway, Margaux Hemingway, Tony Hancock, Brian Epstein, Marilyn Monroe, Clive of India, Cleopatra, Kurt Cobain, Virginia Woolf, Adolf Hitler, Jack London all committed suicide due to serious depressive illness and the list goes on. Apparently depression particularly affects artistic people, although any claims by me in this direction would be considered highly tenuous by my peers! Winston Churchill was a constant sufferer, calling it his "Black Dog".

300 years ago, John Dryden wrote:

"Great wits are sure to madmen near allied " .

"Artistic " Manic depressives (although I am not " Manic " nor "bi-polar") from history included Handel, Berlioz, Schumann, Beethoven, Byron, Bergmann, Mahler, Dante, Shelley, Balzac, our own Stephen Fry and, more recently, the lovely "Bi-Polar " Catherine Zeta -Jones!

It is of course not a socially ACCEPTABLE illness amongst ones Peers like, for example, cancer where you get rather more sympathy. However, it can be just as dangerous a killer, and many are susceptible. Doctors treat more people for depression than ANY other illness- over 3million last year. I now learn that "One in Three " Twenty something"s " are depressed, and suicide now accounts for 20% of all deaths of young people. 20%!

10% of women and some 5-7% of men have been treated for depression at one time or another. That means several of your friends or acquaintances have been treated even if they haven"t mentioned it. Well you wouldn"t would you? Like I said, its such a socially unacceptable, and misunderstood thing. It is said one and a half million people in the UK have descended into becoming anti -depressant pill and tranquillizer junkies, and the NHS spent approximately £230 million last year on these mood altering pills alone. But how effective are these pills?

Interestingly, it is a matter of record that the anti depressant drug generic name "paroxetine " that I happened to be on was, by 2005 raising concern, because according to a group of scientists, far from relieving depression, it was causing many to become suicidal.

Looking back on this experience, I suppose these things shape us and make us stronger assuming we can, in the end, overcome them. "What doesn"t kill you makes you stronger.." as the saying goes. But whatever you do, don"t listen to American Blues singer Billie Holliday"s "Gloomy Sunday". At least 100 suicides have been linked to this very depressing song!

After everything, I feel I"ve had a good and rather privileged life. As I say, there have been worse lives lived. I know. For example, I wasn"t shot "Going over the top " in Ypres, or born in Ethiopia or an "ex-pat " Farmer in Zimbabwe. And can you imagine what life was like living under the Taliban in Afghanistan.Read "The Kite Runner " and "A Thousand splendid suns " if you want to find out.Horrifying, especially for women.

My fitness has remained good enabling me still to play and enjoy tennis and golf, and I would still be playing rugby if I could,whilst the Tree people of Papua New Guinea have to concentrate all their time and effort on hunting for food and constructing primitive shelter. We are indeed privileged   as a race and lucky as a planet full of life whereas all around us in the known universe there is nothing like us so far as we have been able to ascertain. Life has, in many ways, been an adventure and, as you can see , I"ve tried out lots of things, some of which I have taken on and developed satisfactorily, and some, abandoned along the way. A bit of a rollercoaster life lead I suppose, but that"s kept it interesting in a way. As a family, we have had lots of fun over the years, which has been to a degree counter-balanced by some problems and heartaches as discussed. My family can be the judge of how well it all went in the end. In later years, the Missus and I had an unconventional marital relationship by some standards although not unique, and eventually it all ended as I suppose it was destined so to do, but if we were asked, we would advise couples to chose the style and type of relationship that suits them and definitely not be hidebound by convention. Its their marriage, not anyone else"s, after all, although people are quick to interfere or judge you and some would wonder why we did not part long ago. For example, when the children left home.. Interestingly, a sort of consensus around our situation seems to have developed amongst family and friends that the correct decision has been made. At least its an honest position with both of us deciding to end the pretence. Better late than never, I suppose, and we are now free to get on with the rest of our lives, however these may turn out. Life is suddenly exciting again, with new possibilities. I just want top go for it during whatever time I have left and see what happens.

Anyway, in the quest for ever lasting love, it appears the romance quickly fades, which is a shame, it is replaced by something else rather more routine. One recent poll suggests 14 months is the point at which couples stop saying "I Love You". When the wife stops looking after her looks around the house, and the husband starts farting in bed or leaving the lavatory door open. Here is another "how - love - dies" statistic: how the mad, exciting sexual attraction between two people expires after exactly two years, three months and four days. Not cynicism, science. A chemical messenger in the brain called "Nerve growth factor" goes fizzing around at first, bringing fire to your loins and a light in your eyes and then, one day, its burns out, to be replaced,if you"re lucky, by the so called "cuddle hormone ", Oxytocin, which is a bit of an anti–climax, and you end up loving the dog instead!

Nowadays, young people are turning their backs on marriage on the basis they "want to have fun first " which in itself is an indictment suggesting, as it does, that they feel you can"t have fun AND be married. So why get married at all if you feel like that? Currently about a quarter of us are single, people are getting married older, and we are therefore experiencing the lowest marriage rate since 1862. Over 60s divorce rates are currently the only ones rising, which is fascinating news.

True love has, for me, been a fleeting and elusive phenomenon. I have "Loved " any number of times, but only briefly as it turned out, and "In love" perhaps three or four times. As things stood I had been without love for so long that, until recently, I could barely remember what it feels like to truly love someone and to have that love returned. Watching film and TV love stories always made me cry because I knew, deep down, even though married, I was without love. I felt empty. So when, not so long ago and completely unsolicited as I wasn"t looking for anything, love paid me a visit, I was not a little surprised as, to be frank, I had signed off on the possibility of it ever happening again. Sadly, it has not lasted, but was good whilst it did.

For the right two people to meet, so many things need to happen.
The earth turned to bring us together.It turned on itself and in us until it finally brought us together in this dream.

Anyway, moving on.

I feel we brought up two really balanced children who are kind, interesting, always very good company and, so far, successful in their chosen lives . This is probably the best thing to come out of our marriage from both our points of view, and it is good to know we did them proud. They have certainly done us proud.They are both now in their 30s. Sara has an excellent career and has made an excellent marriage to a really good and solid bloke– Myles- a successful and ambitious teacher in the public school system - and Adam has qualifications coming out of his ears. He is now channelling his boundless entrepreneurial enthusiasm and energy into a new property company he has started with friends on the south coast. I support his "going for it" attitude and am sure it will pay off one day soon. Not for him the conventional. I put a lot of their success down to good work on their part, encouragement and discipline on our part when they were young, (partly) financial and other support well targeted, and a lot of love. They are great company and we are as close as a family as we can be given our geographical separation. As I said before , I really miss their company and taking them around even now, and would gladly do all that again, only more so, as the first time around I was all too often absent at work, especially when Sara was younger. One of the few difficulties regarding bringing up the kids - who were generally well behaved, was choosing the right schools for them and then committing to paying school fees, which at times were hard to find even though I was always very well paid. We did try the state school system at primary level, but it didn"t work for us as it wasn"t developing our children"s all round talents like the old grammar schools did and the private system does now. Nevertheless, they both, unlike some children, paid back the investment by working hard and doing very well. They also say they appreciated their schools and the financial sacrifice that went into putting them there. I cannot tell you how pleasing it was to hear that from their own lips. I know for a fact that many Kids do NOT appreciate what their parents have done for them over the years– even resent things - and that must be awful for the parents. Our kids also became, well .....just lovely, kind and generous people.

Sara now has the child so long craved for and deserved - Poppy Nash - and its all good so far. Lets hope this continues. She will be a great Mum.

I am now well into my 60s and still desperately trying to find out who I am. Still trying new things. Life for me has often been a struggle to identify what it is I DO want. I recently signed up for a professional acting/modelling agency to see if I could do something in TV and film. Why not? If you don"t buy a ticket, you can"t enter the lottery, can you? Give it a go, that"s what I say. It should help put off old age, at least for a while.Got to keep going. I"ve done a few auditions for TV Advertisements but am yet to get a part. Amongst one or two other things, including some modelling, I have been a "Support Artiste " in the film "Iron Lady ", about the life of my hero Margaret Thatcher,with Meryl Streep(Thatcher) and Richard E Grant (Heseltine) in whose

"Gang " I am. In the event, I did manage to appear in two scenes in the final "Cut". That said, only a few friends spotted me!

Oh, and I"ve not even talked about the "Good walk spoiled " that is Golf– a very cruel game that I have tampered with for over forty years now and has beaten me more often in that time than I have beaten it! In a way, I wish it had never been invented. Ok its not that bad, but you get my drift. Tennis, on the other hand, at which I am a late starter, rewards me time and time again with an enjoyable and fulfilling few hours.

As it happens, I am not looking forward to either retirement or old age, and as they draw nearer I meet them with some trepidation. The decay of old age comes into stark relief when juxtapositioned with the idyll and youthfulness of, well, youth. At 65 I don"t feel particularly old as it happens, but what have us " Baby Boomers " really got to look forward to as our bodies start to creak and our skin starts to wrinkle up? Certainly nothing like some of the things I have been writing about passim. I suppose what I am searching for now is a place called "Peace of Mind " and I think I might be getting there. I do feel much more relaxed and liberated these days and am enjoying a bit of an "Indian summer" of my life. It seems to me that when you have that, you are ahead in the game. At the moment I don"t need to worry as I have several interesting and time consuming projects on the go that will keep me busy for a few years hopefully. Currently four non - executive positions plus one consultancy helping some people get into Factoring in Africa if you please! That"s more than enough for now thank you.

One thing you CAN put me down for is a little help to die if I get one of those nasty illnesses, for example MND–the idea of being unable to help myself or get around doesn"t appeal I"m afraid.

But is it long life or quality of life that"s the most important? I am clear in my own mind:

There are now 12,000 people over a 100 years of age in this country, compared with only 100 revealed by the 1911 Census. Me? I am only interested in quality of life not quantity of life, and getting to that sort of age holds no appeal whatsoever if I"m honest. The thought of driving one of those little motorised buggies down to the village to get my supplies fills me with horror. Going into a "Care " Home appeals even less.

The life expectancy statistics are interesting though.

If we take the average life expectancy for a man, 77.7 years (in 1911 it was 50 years) we can add or subtract the following years under certain circumstances:

For a "professional " person	Add 3years
For an "unskilled" manual worker	Minus 4 years
Moderate drinker?	Add 1 year
Big Drinker?	Minus 3 years
No drink ?	Minus 1 year!!
Never smoked	Add 3 Years
Men over 5"10"	Add 1 year
Men under 5"8"	Minus 1 year
Living rough	Minus 25 years

A lot depends on where you live as well , as life expectancy is less if you live in poor areas.

Main message? Don"t be poor.

As I say, I do not look forward to full retirement when there will be no more mountains to climb, except trying to overcome illness perhaps, and there are only so many games of golf or tennis that one can, or even wishes, to play in any week, and even those will have to stop in the end when the body is no longer up to it. I suspect reading and travel will come to the fore as I go on and I shall definitely work till I drop , at least up to a point. I will shortly be drawing the State Pension and I must say that will be very welcome after all the years of paying in. Of course, with the Baby Boomer generation just starting to draw their state pensions en masse, the pressure on the Exchequer is going to intensify over the next few years-a fact that"s going to do nothing for an already overburdened State purse,thanks partly to one Gordon Brown"s profligacy in the boom years. Goodness knows what the State is going to be able to afford given copper bottomed public sector employee pensions it also has to support in the years ahead, but I foresee problems. It is good to see the "Coalition" now trying to tackle what will be a controversial issue. However, I shall draw mine such as it is with no conscience, given the hundreds of thousands of pounds I have paid in taxes and NIC over my working life.

Over my lifetime I have had some " Downs " but hey, how can you tell what are "Ups " until you"ve had some "Downs "?? I have given up smoking several times, sometimes more successfully than others, but still indulge, to my shame I suppose, albeit just a few rollups per day. Much cheaper than regular fags and allegedly less chemicals!

Whilst "Carpe Diem " is my favourite expression, I have sometimes, but not always, "Seized the day ", but when I have it has usually worked out well, and its usually better to just have a go so there are no regrets for not trying. Remember– you don"t want to be on your deathbed wishing you had tried this or that or the other thing. Get the things you want to do DONE! Live your life as if every day may be your last day on this Earth. Do it NOW or tomorrow may never come. Ask my friends Roger and Howard–life cut off at the ridiculously early age of 20.

Don"t save yourself for some future promised land. Go for it now. Live in the PRESENT. FUCKING GO FOR IT, GO ON!!

I have learnt that, in life, you should always ask for what you want and I have realised that the worst regrets occur when you look back on something you didn"t try, which you really wanted to try , not when you failed at something you gave a go.

One thing I have learnt is its okay to fail, but its not okay to give up trying. And we should never wish for that which is lost- its not coming back and remember the old Italian proverb:

"It is better to live one day as a lion, than a thousand years as a lamb " although I"m not claiming here that I have quite done so myself.

I have met some fascinating people, have made a few very good friends and many acquaintances, and achieved quite a lot one way or another. There are two kids, at least four excellent and thriving companies and a thriving rugby club still out there that I had a lot to do with!

As they say,

" Prediction can be difficult especially about the future "

but I go forward with some optimism and a general intention to live as full a life as possible. One can do no more.

On our Deathbeds we should all be called to account not by a mythical God, but by ourselves and our friends and family. Did I do my best? Did I live, by and large, a moral Life? Did I actually make a difference in the world? I don"t know so as it"s for others to judge, but I do hope so.

I am not looking forward to old age as it happens, mainly due to the fact that sport plays such a big part in my life so I dread any infirmity that will leave me unable to get around and play my games or look after myself. And I definitely don"t fancy getting Alzheimer"s from all that I have heard about this awful illness.

My Dad had the best way out. "Fit as a butchers dog " for 89 years then suddenly....

Mum was in the bedroom and smelt burning. Investigating, she passed through the kitchen and found the cabbages had boiled dry on the cooker. In a panic, she rushed into the lounge and there was Dad on the floor by the TV, his body contorted. Then calmly, she put a pillow under his head, spoke to him, no reply. He was still breathing, but his face was lop-sided. Having had a serious stroke herself some years earlier, she knew instantly what it was. She called an ambulance and he was taken to the local hospital then rang me. He had an immediate scan. Stroke was confirmed, and it was massive. The Neurologist confirmed there was no hope for him. The family gather at his bedside and a week long vigil begins. He did regain consciousness of a sort for a day or so during which time we were able to tell him we loved him and it would be OK , but he spent the time pulling out any tubes put in him to feed /drugs etc. He knew he was knackered and had clearly determined he was going and didn"t want to be kept alive artificially. Later, loading him up with morphine seemed to become a tacit agreement between us and the Doctors. He then lapsed, mercifully, into the coma from which he never awoke. My Sister, Mum and I had worked shifts at his bedside over the previous days during which his breathing became increasingly quick and laboured. Then, suddenly, a big sigh, and he was gone. I was alright at the funeral– calm and in control– until his coffin turned up at the Milford Church in the hearse. Then I started blubbing like a big kid and only just managed to stay in control to do the eulogy. I still miss him terribly. Mum wasn"t interested in life after Dad went, and after a while in an old folks home she detested, passed away three years later.

One final thing:

Don"t cry for me when the time comes. Celebrate the good times with one of the "Lucky Generation".

Footnote:

I know everyone struggles to sing Robbie Burns "Old Lang Syne" at New Years. Well here"s the English version of the words so you"ll never get stuck again:

Should old acquaintance be forgot,
and never brought to mind ?
Should old acquaintance be forgot,
and old lang syne ?

CHORUS:
For auld lang syne, my dear,
for auld lang syne,
we"ll take a cup of kindness yet,
for auld lang syne.
And surely you"ll buy your pint cup !
and surely I"ll buy mine !
And we"ll take a cup o" kindness yet,
for auld lang syne.

CHORUS
We two have run about the slopes,
and picked the daisies fine ;
But we"ve wandered many a weary foot,
since auld lang syne.

CHORUS
We two have paddled in the stream,
from morning sun till dine† ;
But seas between us broad have roared
since auld lang syne.

CHORUS
And there"s a hand my trusty friend !
And give us a hand o" thine !
And we"ll take a right good-will draught,
for auld lang syne.
CHORUS
etc

No wonder no-one ever gets it right!!